Praise for *Psychi...*

"I have always loved Dr. Michael [astrology, but in this book, he turn... favorite topics: dreams. If you are spiritually curious, you will love this exploration of mystical dreams that are part of the human experience. Intuition and dreams come from the same place, and Michael expertly shows us all the potential ways we can tap into our intuitive sensibility by focusing on what can happen when we're sleeping."

—Colette Baron-Reid, intuitive counselor and host of *Inside the Wooniverse* podcast

"To me, the dream world is the waking world, and the waking world, the dream, and with Dr. Michael's guidance, you'll understand why and take the mystical journey of a lifetime! Dr. Michael shares how the dream world opens your intuition up, plugs you into higher dimensions, and literally transforms your waking world, right before your eyes. He covers it all: shared dreams, visits by deceased loved ones, and even the powerful, *positive*, mystical possibilities hidden in night terrors. How does it get any better than this? If you've ever wanted to know more about the wild things that can happen in your dreams, this book is for you. I give this book a mighty, *mighty* woo-hoo!"

—Michael Sandler, founder of *Inspire Nation* podcast and author of *The Automatic Writing Experience*

Psychic
DREAMER

About the Author

Dr. Michael Lennox (Los Angeles, CA) is a psychologist, astrologer, and expert in dreams and dream interpretation. He has appeared on SyFy, MTV, NBC, and countless radio shows and podcasts, and has published articles in *Today's Woman, TV Guide, Star,* and many other magazines. He teaches classes in self-investigation to a worldwide audience and can be found on social media and in his weekly podcast, *Conscious Embodiment: Astrology and Dreams with Dr. Michael Lennox.* Visit him at www.michaellennox.com.

Psychic
DREAMER

Exploring the Connection between
Dreams and Intuition

DR MICHAEL LENNOX

Llewellyn Publications • Woodbury, Minnesota

FIRST EDITION
First Printing, 2024

Cover design by Kevin R. Brown

Llewellyn Publications is a registered trademark of Llewellyn Worldwide Ltd.

Library of Congress Cataloging-in-Publication Data (Pending)
ISBN: 978-0-7387-7428-2

Llewellyn Worldwide Ltd. does not participate in, endorse, or have any authority or responsibility concerning private business transactions between our authors and the public.

All mail addressed to the author is forwarded but the publisher cannot, unless specifically instructed by the author, give out an address or phone number.

Any internet references contained in this work are current at publication time, but the publisher cannot guarantee that a specific location will continue to be maintained. Please refer to the publisher's website for links to authors' websites and other sources.

Llewellyn Publications
A Division of Llewellyn Worldwide Ltd.
2143 Wooddale Drive
Woodbury, MN 55125-2989
www.llewellyn.com

Printed in the United States of America

Other Books by Dr. Michael Lennox

Dream Sight:
A Dictionary and Guide for Interpreting Any Dream
(Llewellyn, 2011)

Llewellyn's Complete Dictionary of Dreams
(Llewellyn, 2015)

Llewellyn's Little Book of Dreams
(Llewellyn, 2017)

Acknowledgments

This book would not have been possible without the participation of so many dreamers. I thank them all for sharing so openly with me. Special thank you to Lorraine, who was the best gentle reader ever, and to my team, without whom nothing gets done (thank you Lisa, Paisley, Jonathan, Zo, and Eddie).

Contents

Introduction

Everyone is intuitive.

This begs the question "What is intuition?"

Merriam-Webster defines intuition as "the power or faculty of attaining to direct knowledge or cognition without evident rational thought and inference." In other words, intuition is an experience of knowing, but rather than it coming from outside evidence of what we are declaring we know, we have an inner sense of understanding that something can be true or so because we can feel it. Intuition is a form of perception, but one that sits apart from the rational, thinking mind that governs how we perceive the world around us. That thinking mind is the voice that you identify as your Self, the part of you that knows who you are and where you are. "I think, therefore I am" is the famous phrase by Descartes that aptly describes this construct, based on the belief that the narrating voice in your head is how you guide yourself through your life. But what about other forms of perception?

We often think of our intuition as being a still, small voice inside of us that is, ultimately, difficult to hear and even more challenging to respond to and honor when it whispers bits of intuitive guidance in our ears. The voice that is our narrator is almost impossible to turn off or even diminish in volume enough to hear that still, small voice. And while everyone has a different experience of what might be called the "inner monologue," it is safe to assume that the way we all relate to ourselves in this way is rational, and perhaps even literal. We talk to ourselves in our mind, and that inner conversation eclipses all other forms of perception.

Something happens when we go to sleep. The rational, thinking part of our perception goes to sleep with our conscious awareness. For somewhere between six and nine hours a night on average, we drift into another realm entirely, overtaken by the sweet death of sleep. We are reborn each morning as our brain fires back up and our thinking mind turns on almost instantaneously, and we are back to the orientation we are familiar with: I think, therefore I am. Not so during sleep. As we move through the various stages of sleep, dropping down, lower and lower, into a place deep inside our psyche where we are deeply connected to existence itself, reality drops away and we enter the realm of dreams, where anything can happen and probably will. The rational mind is sleeping, and so that still, small voice opens up and sings loudly in the form of dreams. As a result, our ability to connect to our intuition increases exponentially, and many people report connecting to dreams that offer experiences of *precognition*, or dreaming of things that have not yet happened but will occur in the future.

My very first dream memory is from when I was three years old, and it absolutely was a mystical dream. In the dream, I found myself in a kind of empty space. Years later I saw the movie *The Matrix*, and there is a scene where the two main characters find themselves inside the program of the Matrix itself, before anything has been loaded in. My dream was very much like that, where I was in this vast, empty landscape and the only thing I was physically aware of was me in my little body. I had an awareness that above me was something of enormity and below me was a sense of infinitesimal smallness, and this was absolutely terrifying. The dream felt like a nightmare, but it was also this intensity that caused the dream to be imported into my psyche. I had the dream enough times to have it burned into my memory in a way that I can still feel to this day.

As an adult, I was easily able to see this as a dream of the nature of infinity, and it was, in some ways, my first anchor into the consciousness that has driven me my entire life. Exploring the mystery has been, it turns out, the most powerful motivator for everything I have ever done, even above some of the early desires I had for my life. My three-year-old psyche had no sense of what the unfolding of my life might look like, but my higher self may have sent me this dream as a kind of initiation into consciousness itself.

I don't recall where I was when I first made the association between what the solar system looks like and the model of an atom, where a central hub is orbited by tiny particles. I do remember being gobsmacked at the idea that something enormous and something so impossibly small could reflect each other, and I can remember talking about it with my science-driven mother when I was a teenager. This notion was just mind-blowing to me, but it would still be a few years before I made the connection to it with my early dream.

Cut to a little over a decade later, and I found myself living in Los Angeles and in my very first workshop on dreams and dream interpretation. During the first session of that workshop, we were all asked to share with the group how and why we were interested in our dreams, and I told the story of my three-year-old dream. For the first time since having this dream, I found myself describing it. In so doing, I made the connection between the sensation of that early dream, the association with the molecule and solar system replication, and the idea that diving into the world of my dreams might deepen the spiritual path that I was now on in earnest. It wasn't long before I was offering the first workshop of my own, and I had my first actual client by the time I reached my early thirties.

I have been working with dreams for over forty years at the time of this writing. I have had many of the experiences that are cataloged within these pages, and I have tried to throw in some science, where I know it, and some mystical background, where I have some knowledge. Thanks to social media, I am now surrounded by thousands of dreamers. I called upon them to share their dreams with you in these pages, which has allowed me to hear about people's firsthand experiences and present them for you here. I trust that you will be inspired and perhaps be a bit curious to see what might be possible in your own dream life to develop your connection to life's mysteries.

Indeed, we are all intuitive, and many people have a strong desire to develop and expand their intuitive capacity. The more masterfully we tap into the still, small voice of guidance that is inside of us, the more graceful life becomes, because as our intuition grows, we become more effective at tapping into a flow state. Because we are the most immediately connected to this inner wisdom when we are sleeping, paying attention to and working with our dreams is perhaps the most direct and powerful way to deepen our access to this inner wisdom in our waking life as well. Your dreams are waiting to help you on this journey, so dive on in to the pages that follow, and as I like to say, *have at it!*

Chapter One

Precognitive Dreaming

In order to understand the idea of the dream state opening us up to precognitive information, it is best if we get on the same page with some vocabulary about how to talk about what precognition is, and how we are to understand the premonitions that rise up seemingly out of nowhere. It is fairly common to conceive of our existence as human beings as a multidimensional experience, and the science of quantum physics has made this notion something we can if not understand exactly, then at least trust that there is such a thing, so the scientists tell us. The mystics understand that there are ways that all people can live simultaneously in both worlds, fully ensconced in this three-dimensional existence that is driven by time, where we only move forward, but also connected to the fourth-dimensional experience, where time is not a factor. Our whole lives exist from first breath to last in some other energetic sensibility that is not of the here and now, but is just as accessible to us, though some are more sensitive about perceiving this than others.

A Multidimensional World

One of the easiest ways to understand this distinction of different dimensions is to consider how we in the three-dimensional world relate to a world that is two-dimensional. Our three-dimensional world has height, width, and depth. We regularly create two-dimensional consciousness in a manner that, because of the internet and social media and everyone walking around with a high-quality camera in their pocket, is a constant and consistent element of modern culture. When you take a picture, draw an image, write some words, or create a TikTok video, you are creating two-dimensional expressions that you can easily hold in your three-dimensional body. Now just up that notion to this idea of a dimension of us that is greater than who we are, that is not limited by having to move through chronology but knows our entire existence from beginning to end.

This is how I personally define the *soul*, as the consciousness of our life in its entirety. We are born into a body and begin the trek through our life from first breath to last. That first and last breath are known to this higher-self aspect of who we are, and as we move through our life, the creations of our day-to-day existence generate a life. That life, the life you live, is like the TikTok video of your fourth-dimensional self. We are always connected to this aspect of consciousness, where part of us knows every moment of our life from beginning to end. A person who has a psychic gift, then, is an individual who has the ability to tap into this fourth dimension of consciousness, where the veil between what has happened and what will happen is thin. Such people can sit in ordinary space while part of them visits extraordinary space, and they can tell us what they see, feel, and know.

We can all tap into this fourth dimension at a fundamental level. It's a little bit like singing, though. Everyone who can speak can sing, for singing is technically just sustained sound of the voice on pitch. Yes, everyone can sing, but without a good ear for matching tone, the singing will not be a pleasant experience for the listener. In this same way, we can all feel in some way our connection to this fourth dimension, but some people have more talent in their ability to tap into that realm than others. Everyone's intuitive ability can be increased and amplified with discipline and practice, but it is in our dreams that we are already connected to that consciousness, if for no other reason than the thinking mind that would negate such intuitive input is fast asleep, leaving the larger part of our unconscious perceptions to marinate in that invisible veil between worlds.

It is often said that time is an illusion, but that's not really accurate. Time simply *is*, and that's no fantasy. We move through time, and the body is where that movement is focused. But we each have a mind that is designed to perceive the world of time as we move through it. The mind can move into the past and into the future, even with our body stuck in the present time. This is how we plan what comes next while we are learning from the past. But our minds are extraordinarily limiting, especially when it comes to the intuitive process of tapping into the guidance that comes from these other, higher dimensions.

The mind is the only way we can perceive anything in our waking life, but the mind is also not to be trusted. Most people either ignore their intuition or get confused by all the sensations in their mind and body, and often do not know how to trust what their intuition is telling them. You have heard this before and have probably said it yourself: "My instincts told me to _____, but I ignored them." Those instincts are our intuition in action, coming from the part of us that is fourth-dimensional, where time is irrelevant. In waking life, most people are shut off from the ability to perceive such a subtle energetic piece of information, partly because the rational mind rejects them. When we are asleep and dreaming, that rational mind is also asleep, and we are much freer to have experiences out of time, through an experience we call *precognitive dreaming*.

Precognitive Dreams Revealed

When I was seventeen years old, I had a dream. It was innocuous enough. I was at my high school, but not in a way that was readily recognizable; I had a dreamlike sense that this was where I was. The main image of the dream was that I was sitting on the floor, legs crossed, in a circle with others who were sitting the same way. That was it. I was an avid dreamer and relished in the process of waking up each day and ruminating over the rich landscapes I would visit during my sleep. This was one dream image of thousands that would float through my thoughts, since I had such an active dream life and I thought of them with some reverence. I had not yet started journaling about my dreams; that would come with adulthood. My fascination with dreams started in those teenage years.

About a week later, I walked into my dance rehearsal that I had every day during the last two years of high school. We had a very comprehensive program for dance and a gym teacher who had been a dancer in her younger years, and this dance company was one of the many creative endeavors that carried me through a difficult adolescence. There was some drama that had arisen in the ranks of the company, and that day we walked in and Miss Hicks wanted us to sit down and have a group discussion. She invited us to sit on the floor, and we did so, spreading out into a large circle of students sitting cross-legged—just like in my dream. It took a few minutes for me to realize that the image from my dream almost exactly matched what was happening in my waking life at that moment, to the point that I felt like there was a powerful intuitive connection being established. I didn't have the language for it at the time, but now I understand that it was my first precognitive dream.

As I did my research for this book, what I found was that there is a kind of precognitive dreaming that is common and touches many people, at least a little. These sorts of dreams, which include premonitions of events that follow in waking life, are relatively innocuous. I remember a client many years ago who described a dream in which she was sitting cross-legged in a circle of women who were also in the same seated position. A week or so after the dream, she found herself at a meditation event, and lo and behold, it was a circle of women and they were all asked to sit in lotus position, cross-legged in a circle. She was gobsmacked when she noticed this. In the grand scheme of things, this clearly wasn't a life-changing dream experience, but it did confirm that being in the dream state can blur the boundaries of our waking-life experience of time unfolding in a linear fashion, which is one of the ways intuition works.

In the spirit of premonition dreams being a kind of rudimentary way of tapping into intuitive guidance, dreamer Kristy reminded me of an important distinction that many people experience. She told me, "Yes, I have regular pre-cog dreams; however, I don't realize they were pre-cog until it is happening [in real life], and then it is as if everything slows down and I just let things happen. I have tried to intervene and change what is going to happen [in real life]; however, everything goes sideways, so I learned my lesson and just be still in the moments that pass." This relaxed way of witnessing your dreams is important as you seek to have a deeper relationship with them, and sometimes it's just about trusting the way the unconscious and conscious minds work with each other.

These premonition dreams are quite common, where something happens in a dream scenario and that same experience shows up in waking life the next day or soon after. Although this is a common and universal experience of such intuitive dreams, it is possible that many people have such experiences but do not notice them because they are not paying close enough attention to their dreams. There is a population of humans whose capacity for tapping into psychic information through dreams transcends a sense of premonition. These *bona fide* precognitive dreamers experience a more literal connection to dreams that predict the future. Such gifts are often thought to be intergenerational, and it is not uncommon for people to report that siblings, parents, and grandparents all have some version of the same gift.

Dreamer Linda reported to me that although she has had many premonition dreams throughout her life, this has changed for her over the years: "Since I quit being stubborn, I do not have them much anymore, as I get an intuitive visual instead." This is an interesting reflection that, as we grow in age and wisdom, we can also become more attuned to our intuitive nature. Like many people who are oriented to having such dream experiences, Linda shared her top three with me.

The first big premonition dream that Linda remembered was a repeated dream where she was driving in heavy traffic. In fact, she was driving close to seventy miles per hour in the middle lane. All of a sudden, the traffic in front of her stopped and she slammed on the brakes, but her brakes did not work, and then she woke up quite suddenly. This dream occurred three times over a short period of time in exactly the same way: driving fast in traffic, a sudden stop to negotiate, and brakes that failed. Though in waking life her truck was running fine and there was no indication that there was any sort of problem, Linda took her vehicle to the mechanic. He ended up diagnosing a pretty serious problem that, he indicated, was usually only discovered when the brakes would inevitably fail. Linda was able to preemptively fix this problem that might otherwise have led to a much more dangerous scenario.

In another instance, a dream of driving to work included a large truck that pulled out right in front of her. Linda slammed into the side of this large vehicle and died in the dream, which, she reported, was very vivid. That morning, Linda told her husband about the dream before she left for work. When she reached the intersection where the dream accident had occurred, she slowed down to be extra careful. She was rewarded indeed when the very truck from her dream ran through the stop sign, but Linda was prepared. If she hadn't slowed down, the dream would have actualized, and she might not be here to tell the tale.

When Linda shared her third big premonition dream with me, she added something that is crucial to understand about such dream experiences because it sets them apart from other, more typical dreams. Linda reported that these dreams, at some point after having had enough of them, began to "feel familiar." This language is important, for although such distinctions may be quite subtle, they are absolute. Standard dreams feel a certain way, but mystical dreams have different sensations, as we are discussing here and will explore in some other chapters in this book as well. Because Linda had been paying such close attention to her dreams for much of her life, after a time she began to make this distinction. This allowed her to pay closer attention to such dreams when they came, hence her willingness to call a mechanic even though her waking-life car seemed just fine.

Precognitive Dreaming Can Start Very Young

For Elizabeth, the experience of precognitive dreams began at a very young age. An active and vivid dreamer from the get-go, she expressed to me, "I learned early on to pay attention to my dreams. And often my dreams are so intense, I have no choice but to pay attention," a sentiment I personally identify with. Though no one in her family has ever reported having this same ability, some members of her clan have had significant dreams of connecting with loved ones who have passed over, so her family environment offered the context for powerful dreaming experiences.

Although Elizabeth told me that she can't remember exactly when these dreams started, because it was early on in life, the first story she shared with me was a dream she had just before starting school. She dreamt of a classroom in which she was playing with another little girl, and the two of them got in trouble for not paying attention to the teacher. Sure enough, when school started in real life, five-year-old Elizabeth met the exact little girl from her dream and they got into some trouble for not listening, just like what had happened in her dream. A few years later, Elizabeth had a dream that she was on her way home from school. In the dream, she was near her mailbox, walking home from the bus stop, and the friend who lived on the next street came running toward her, frantically yelling her name. Elizabeth described it like this:

> I was 7 or 8 and I had a dream that I was by my mailbox walking home from the bus stop and my friend who lived on the next street over came running down the street yelling my name. She was frantic and yelling something about my brother. As she got closer, I realized that she was telling me he was hurt and I needed to come quick. I looked toward my house and that was it. Either the dream transitioned or I just don't remember the rest.

Elizabeth was still a child, and although this was an experience she had already begun to have, her childhood self simply brushed this off as a typical dream, and she never mentioned it to anyone or thought about it again. A few months later, when the dream was long in the rearview mirror of her memory, there came a day when she was standing by her mailbox, coming from the bus stop, and the friend from the other street came around the corner, yelling frantically about something. Although the friend was not yelling about Elizabeth's brother, the memory of the dream came flooding back to Elizabeth at that moment. With that, she ran to her house to search for her mother to tell her about this very strong feeling that something was terribly wrong. And indeed, a horrible car accident had occurred, leaving her brother in a coma for weeks, and his recovery included learning how to walk again.

Elizabeth is a prolific precognitive dreamer, and so many of her dreams follow a similar pattern of featuring slice-of-life images that show up in waking life a few days, weeks, or months later. One dream about a random girl seemed fairly innocuous until several months later, when that very girl showed up as a coworker where Elizabeth was working, and that coworker wound up playing an important role in Elizabeth's life at that time. Another work-related dream Elizabeth had as an adult was a similar snapshot of a supervisor, who a year later turned out to be the interviewer in part of Elizabeth's job search. A series of random dream images of a house turned out to be the very house Elizabeth and her husband moved into a few months later. Even the passing of her mother showed up in the dream state before the actual end. In that dream, Elizabeth was watching from above, and when her mother made her transition in waking life, it played out exactly as Elizabeth had dreamed it.

Like so many people who are naturally immersed in their dream life, Leonora explains that she has always had vivid dreams, so much so that in her early life she began to refer to them as experiences rather than just dreams. She is one of those people who, by virtue of her own experience, has the sense that dreams are, in some ways, more real than waking life. She says, "Since I was a child, I have always said that my dreams are more real than the life I live when my eyes are open." During the years that I was working on this book, there were two major world events that were a prominent part of the collective landscape. One was, of course, the pandemic and the spread of COVID-19. Another was the war in Ukraine. Leonora got a glimpse of both of these events before they happened in her dream experiences.

About a month before the pandemic began, Leonora had a dream where a huge black cloud of dust covered the entire world. In this landscape, she had a very strong feeling that people needed to connect in love, that it was important to connect with loved ones and give them all a hug. In the dream narrative, she knew that "we had to get together with our loved ones and 'dance' before it was too late to do so." She describes this dream image as being so vivid that she woke knowing there was some measure of truth to it. In fact, she went to the supermarket the next day and started to tell people to hug each other and to go visit the people they love because they would not be able to do this for a long time. Of course, on that day she just looked like a goofy lady in the grocery store. But a month after this experience, COVID-19 began, the world shut down, and indeed, it was a while before we got to hug and dance with our loved ones.

When dreamer Sandra was in her early thirties, she began her spiritual journey by studying with a local mystery school that not only introduced her to the principles that she would use to contextualize her entire life, but also connected her to a powerful group of like-minded people who were on a healing journey of their own. This was a rich and vibrant time in her life, where she was both newly married and just beginning her career as a mental health professional. At the time of one particular dream, the biggest challenge Sandra was facing was a difficult journey with infertility. Several invasive treatment protocols as well as two devastating miscarriages were making this a particularly difficult part of Sandra's life journey. This is how she described one dream:

> I dreamt that I was sitting in a park on a lovely sunny day. On a hill a short distance from me, I overheard three women from my healing school discussing my situation. I knew two of the women, but I did not recognize a third woman with blonde hair. They were reviewing all aspects of my struggle to become a mother (on the physical, mental, emotional, and spiritual levels) and making suggestions from the energy healing point of view. I felt as if I was overhearing a loving "treatment team." Suddenly, the woman with blonde hair that I did not know walked over to me and said, "If you ever want to come see me about this situation, here is my business card." I remember holding her shiny white card in my hand, and the dream ended.

Now here's where the precognitive piece comes in. Much to Sandra's surprise, or perhaps not at all surprisingly, a short time after this dream, she found herself in her usual class at the mystery school. Only on this particular day, a woman with blonde hair in the audience caught her attention, and given the permissiveness of the environment, Sandra had no trouble going up to this woman and saying, "I know this is kind of odd, but I had this dream where you handed me your business card and told me to come see you. What do you do for a living?" The woman laughed and said that she was an energy healer, and gave Sandra her business card for the second time, only this time in the corporeal world.

Sandra immediately made an appointment with this woman and continued to see her regularly for a time. This was Sandra's first experience with energy healing, and perhaps that made it even more powerful. She describes the work they did as being very deep and profound. Sandra was able to identify core patterns of wounds, both present-life wounds and what she described as past-life difficulties, and through this work, she moved through some powerful transformation and healing. Alas, becoming a mother through birth was not to be part of Sandra's journey, but this deep work was part of the healing process that allowed her to release her struggles, make peace with her body, and enter into motherhood with more grace. This included a healing ceremony involving a circle of amazingly supportive women, which Sandra can vividly recall to this day.

A third miscarriage followed. The journey to adoption was next on the list, and though this blonde woman healer who first appeared to Sandra in a dream was not around for the completion of the journey that resulted in Sandra's very happy life as a mother, that connection was the key that opened up her healing. Sandra had her dream, and her willingness to take a risk saying hello to the woman from her dream that first day was a reflection of Spirit leading Sandra through her life. Such dreams have the power to offer us precognitive information that may be crucial for the decisions we make that are, ultimately, life-changing.

One of the most active and prolific precognitive dreamers I know is a woman I connected with in a dream circle that I operated for a number of years in the local Los Angeles cancer community. Years ago, I naturally began to attract people in my work who were on a cancer journey. At a certain point I had amassed enough practical experience working with people in such an intense process that I proposed a monthly dream circle to a local well-funded organization that provides wellness care to people in this population. I facilitated this deeply powerful gathering for several years, and one of the people who was a devoted regular was a woman with a strong gift for precognitive dreaming. Her gift for such psychic dreams is strong, but her story of coming into acceptance of this gift is, to me, just as interesting as the fascinating dream experiences that she consistently has as a result of this gift.

Dawna's story started with her grandfather, who was someone who had this precognitive dreaming gift as well. Instead of nurturing these intuitive, mystical experiences, Dawna's grandfather encouraged her to shut these experiences off. When she was five years old, Dawna had her tonsils taken out, a fairly standard operation at the time, when chronic throat infections were often solved by the surgical removal of pieces of tissue that are filled with white blood cells and are part of the body's immune system. In the process of going through this surgery, five-year-old Dawna had a rough moment where her body hemorrhaged and she experienced fever and delirium. This radical physical shakeup resulted in an out-of-body experience in which Dawna felt intuitively that she was being taken care of and was surrounded by angels.

Dawna's grandparents were her primary caretakers in those early years, as Dawna's parents both worked, and care of the children was often provided by this older generation. It was natural, then, for Dawna to describe the experience she had to her grandfather. "I saw angels," Dawna told her grandfather with wonder. He put his finger to his lips in that gesture that says to be quiet. In the conversation that ensued, her grandfather encouraged Dawna to keep very quiet about such phenomena. He shared that he too had such experiences, and had his entire life. He warned that if you spoke about such phenomena with people who did not share your experience, not only would they misunderstand, but they would also probably think you were a weird oddball. Dawna took this warning to heart, and it was over forty years before she opened up to this powerful spiritual gift. It was just waiting to be awakened, which did indeed happen in her early sixties, almost six decades later.

When Dawna was around sixty-three, she was diagnosed with cancer. Moving through a cancer diagnosis is perhaps one of the most brutal of human experiences. Of course, the media constantly inundate us with stories of amazing heroism, where people meet such devastating news in a brave way and come out the other side radically transformed. Many people do not rise up in a movie-of-the-week sort of way, but are rightly pummeled by a body that betrays them, and engage in a dance with mortality that can lead to tremendous psychological and emotional break-downs. There are heroic stories as well, and Dawna's is one of them. Getting cancer, and moving through the healing journey directed by it, was the making of her.

When I discussed this with her in consideration of how, at a very young age, Dawna had made the decision to deny an enormous part of her personal humanity for the sake of other people's perspectives, she said, "After having cancer, I don't give a fuck, you know? The cancer strips away that barrier. Either it makes you a victim and you withdraw, or it's like you say, 'The hell with it, this is who I am.'" She went on to speak of the impact of the dream circle I was facilitating, and added, "And then you have people like you, who through that dream circle was like, 'Oh my god, there are other people having similar experiences.'" By the time I met Dawna, she was on the other side of her diagnosis and treatment and was living fully out loud, completely embracing her intuitive gifts. Her precognitive dreams, which would occasionally focus on people in the circle, became a significant element of this community that met once a month.

For the purposes of this book, I reached out to Dawna to have a more intimate conversation about her precognitive dreaming experiences. She indeed cited her cancer diagnosis as the most profoundly important experience of her life, one that drew a metaphorical line in the sand of before and after. "It was like my life epiphany. The first step is that you get diagnosed and you go down Alice's rabbit hole. And you tumble and you tumble and you tumble. And I wanted to climb out, and I finally realized I can't climb out, I'm in another world." Once Dawna surrendered herself to this new, strange world that she found herself in, she indeed began to feel a powerful sense of expansion. Her spiritual awakening hit every aspect of her life, and though she is now cancer-free and living large in her seventies, her spiritual life opened up only recently, but is an important part of how she lives her life now.

Precognitive dreams are different from typical dreams in terms of feeling, sensation, and, depending on the dream, certain types of structure. Very often, like other mystical dreams you will read about in later chapters, precognitive dreams are more singular and focused in terms of setting a scene. They are often single images that tell a story, as opposed to the lengthy and circuitous dreamlike narratives we are used to. For Dawna, the signal that a precognitive dream has arrived shows up in how she feels when she wakes up after such a dream. "When I wake up after a precognitive dream, even when it's been a perplexing dream image, I'm clearheaded and alert and I jump out of bed. I *feel* those dreams in my bones." This is very different from her typical morning sluggishness, which doesn't usually lift until after her first cup of morning coffee.

I asked Dawna to share with me some of the early dreams she had after this uncanny spiritual awakening that came along with her cancer journey. One of the first precognitive dreams that she recalled had to do, ultimately, with the death of her own mother, who, after a series of strokes, surgeries, and the onset of vascular dementia, had been in an agitated state of decline for a number of weeks. Dawna describes her mother as living "between two worlds" during this time. During this period, her mother was in a fugue (a temporary state of memory loss), though she did respond to her favorite music. There were only a few brief cognizant verbal exchanges, in which Dawna could feel an impulse that there might be something to say out loud that might put her mother at ease or help her release her body in this end-of-life process. One night, Dawna had this dream:

> I dreamt that Mom was 4 to 5 years old. She's wearing a pink floral with green leaves on ivory background cotton dress, with short sleeves and full skirt. She is walking hand-in-hand with her papa in a beautiful park, with lots of lush greenery—trees and bushes, lots of colorful flowers. They are smiling widely at each other, radiantly happy, and excitedly talking, talking, talking.

Dawna woke up feeling pretty refreshed that morning, although she didn't recognize it at the time as being salient to this dream experience. When she was sufficiently roused, she went to her mother's bedside, sat down, and took her hand, stroked her forehead, and gently told her to take her papa's hand and go for a walk in the park, because it was a beautiful day for a walk in the park. Dawna described what happened next like this: "She squeezed my hand and smiled. I knew she understood. She took a deep breath and her body finally relaxed. No more struggles." She died peacefully two days later.

Very often, the precognitive themes expressed in Dawna's dreams are revealed in a series of dreams that play out over a short period of time. In this next example, Dawna had four different dreams that were all related to a dear friend of hers named Harvey, a brilliant man who was not only a writer, poet, and philosopher in his own right, but also a scientist by profession. The connection between this man and Dawna was particularly vibrant in an intellectual way, as they shared through friendship a delight in conversation and connecting on the many topics that they both found fascinating.

Over a two-week period one summer, Dawna had four dreams in which she and Harvey were sitting together, facing forward, on a contemporary gray sofa in some sort of a living room with high ceilings, bare white walls, and a beautiful polished hardwood floor of gleaming taupe. She can even remember the pale gray crewneck cashmere sweater and light-colored pants that Harvey was wearing. And because the setting and outfit were exactly the same in each of these four dreams that played out over two weeks' time, the image was emblazoned in Dawna's memory.

Each dream featured the same, or at least a similar, conversation between them. Each of the scenarios began with Harvey asking the question "Have you heard the quiet?" These dialogues were specific, and Dawna has the receipts, because she had been actively journaling about her dream experiences from the moment her cancer diagnosis changed her life. Each dream featured this sort of back-and-forth, with only slight variations. In the first dream, Harvey asked, "Have you heard the quiet?"

Dawna replied, "Yes."

Harvey continued: "Have you spoken with the quiet?"

To which Dawna added, "Yes, it's my friend."

In each dream, Harvey asked this question over and over again in exactly the same words: *Have you heard the quiet?*

While Dawna's response was slightly different with each iteration of the ask, Harvey repeated the same basic question over and over again, as if he had no other option of expressing himself intellectually at that point. In one dream, she told him she'd been having long talks with the quiet, and in another, she explained that the quiet was always with her. Dawna was baffled by this series of dreams, and so was Harvey when Dawna reached out to share with him this curious phenomenon that was visiting her, clearly attempting to communicate something whose meaning was just out of reach.

Harvey was diagnosed with dementia a year later. He and his wife went to Los Angeles, where Dawna lives, for a visit soon after this diagnosis. They were staying at a rental in Venice, and Dawna was surprised when she entered the space. The polished hardwood floors gleamed, the bare white walls and high ceilings offered a sense of expansiveness, and there in the living room was the gray couch in her dreams—and, of course, Harvey was wearing light khaki pants and a crewneck cashmere sweater. Though his dementia was already expressing itself, he still had enough cognizance at the time to remember the series of dreams Dawna had shared with him the year before. They were able to speak of this, and Harvey was able to share with Dawna that her dreams, and the memory of them, gave him some peace as he moved through this very difficult life transition.

Two last little tidbits about Dawna and her precognitive gift and my experience of it are personal. In the process of working on this book, I hit a wall during the initial writing. This is not uncommon, as the creative process is mysterious and at times frustrating, and when one bumps into resistance, there is no option but to deal with whatever the birthing process requires. I came out of that little bump in the road with an idea to focus specifically on this chapter, and to set up an interview with Dawna as a kind of anchor to the new approach I was intending on using. The first thing Dawna shared with me in that interview was a precognitive-style dream of me, in which she said I was boxing and preparing for a fight. The timing of this dream was exactly concomitant with the private boxing match I was having with this book at that time. And several years ago, Dawna had a precognitive dream in which I was getting married. I am still on the lookout for the husband who might be coming my way, something I trust as a possibility since it has already appeared in Dawna's precognitive dreaming landscape.

This next example is a perfect dream to share in this chapter, but it really came out of my research for the chapter on shared dreaming (chapter 3), which is when two people have some version of the same dream at the same time. This family experience described to me by Christy, a woman in her mid-forties, centers around the passing of the mother, where every sibling had a dream of premonition of her pending death. Here is a setup of precognitive dreams within a family system, at a time of crisis brought on by a death in the family.

Christy was in her mid-forties when her mother was diagnosed with terminal cancer. She has two siblings, brothers both, and they are close in age. The dream she had, and the ones reported by both brothers, all took place within a week of their mother's passing, though Christy's experience occurred literally in the few days when her mother was leaving her body. There are two things to note about Christy, one being that her father made his transition seventeen years earlier, so he was already on the other side when his still-living wife was making her exit. The other is that Christy has had a lifelong fear of tornadoes. Thank you, Dorothy and the Wizard of Oz!

> So, my dad, who had been passed for seventeen-ish years, came to me in the dream and said that I needed to get ready, "the cyclone was coming." That specific word, because I wrote that down, well, the cyclone, that made me think about, like, Dorothy. And what was funny was that in the dream, whenever I'd dream of my dad, he would be in the same clothes, so he had the same outfit on. But my older brother was in the dream, but distracted, like on his phone, and not paying any attention at all, which gave me the sense that he was already aware that our mother was passing. Then my dad gave me a specific time that my mother would pass.

As she recalled the dream, Christy remembered that the time of death her father gave was 4:14 a.m., and there were other details he offered, and his demeanor in the dream was somber. But the presence of her brother in the dream seemed like a significant detail, so it was natural for her to bring it up in conversation the next morning. She spoke with her brother about this, saying, "I had this dream with Dad last night, and you were in it and seemed to know all about what was happening with him." He took this in and replied, "Yeah, he came last week. He told me she would die on December 5th."

It gets even better when you bring the younger brother into the mix. This older brother's participation in Christy's dream made some sense to her, as she recognizes that he has a fairly strong intuition and has an innate connection to the more mystical aspects of life. She does describe him as primarily rational and structure-oriented, as he is an engineer and values rationality over the spiritual, although, when pressed, he will acknowledge that life is filled with mystery. Her younger brother has intellectual limitations, so his perceptions of life are limited in some ways, but clearly not when it comes to connecting to the mysteries. A powerful moment with her younger brother took place when Christy showed up at the hospice later that same morning.

While Christy's younger brother functions well without much support, their mother was naturally concerned about this child in particular, often wondering how well he would be cared for after she was gone. This is a key piece to have in mind when considering what this younger brother had to say that very significant morning: "I had a dream about Dad last night and he said that she [their mother] is gonna wake up this morning and he needs me to tell her that I'm going to be okay and that you guys are going to take care of me."

And true to form, this younger brother's precognitive dream sent him into action. After many days of being in and out of consciousness in a semicomatose state, the mother woke up that day just long enough for this young man to connect with her. As soon as he saw that she was alert, he excitedly told her, "Mom, I'm gonna be okay. Timmy and Christy are gonna help me. I love you and it'll be okay." And with that, she closed her eyes, lay down more peacefully, and passed away that night.

Chapter Two
Lucid Dreaming

Just about everyone has had the experience of lucid dreaming at least once. You are asleep and dreaming, and within the context of the dream experience there is the awareness that you are, in fact, dreaming. The universal experience I am describing is usually reported as something innocuous, almost slipped into the narrative that is playing out in the dream. There you are in some crazy, chaotic storyline in the way most dreams feel, and then this sidebar thought drops in: "Oh wow, I'm dreaming. This is a dream!" This awareness doesn't shift the dream experience. It is almost as if a narrator's voice has slipped into the process, and this uncanny recognition is accepted as perfectly natural. The dream simply continues to unfold, but now there is this tiniest bit of conscious awareness that you are not in your waking-life experience.

There is an illusion that because the waking mind is diminished in our dream consciousness, the narrating voice that we rely on so completely to help us move about our lives is shut off completely as we dream. Then dreaming ends, we wake up, and this conscious awareness fires back on once again. But it is not quite that simple, as by now you are starting to understand. There isn't a clear line between our conscious awareness being turned on or off, like a switch with only two settings. We are most vulnerable to dangers in the world when we are asleep, so we have the built-in capacity for that part of our awareness to be roused in an instant, and with a little chemical jolt, we can go from deep sleep to wide awake in the time that is needed to take a single breath. But outside of that extreme, the process is a little blurrier.

For reasons we are not completely aware of, the brain shuts down that part of our awareness, and this is what allows dreaming to be so profoundly expansive in dimensions that are greater than what our conscious awareness usually allows. This fascinating experience of conscious awareness rising up while the dream state is in full expression is something that is universal indeed. In fact, I can say with some certainty that I have never had anyone express to me that they have never had this lucid awareness while in the dream state at least once. What this tells us is that this separation between conscious awareness and unconscious expansion in the dream state is fluid and loose and can be increased and strengthened, like any mental muscle.

There are three levels of lucid dreaming that I have noted both in my own personal experience and in spending a lifetime listening to dreamers tell of their experiences. The first level is the one already described, where the dreaming landscape gets peppered with little thoughts of conscious awareness, like "I think I'm dreaming." This can happen in tiny little ways, such as just a single thought dropping in at one moment in the dream's unfolding. This awareness can be much more prominent, and dreams can feature this sidebar awareness in much greater volume.

However, this slow amplification of lucid thoughts while you are dreaming occurs because you, the dreamer, are actually beginning to wake up, and the dream state reflects this acceleration toward wakeful consciousness. Within the dream state itself, this can show up as coming to a place where the awareness of your lucidity is so great that you feel a curiosity about what you might do with this budding awareness. Then you wake up. The reported experience might go something like this: "I realized I was dreaming, and then I felt this so acutely that I figured I could use this to control what might happen next in my dream, but then I woke up." The burgeoning consciousness that was present because the dreamer was waking up enters the dream state, and it seems like the lucidity itself ends the dream.

Is This the Dream Life—or Just Reality?

I met Lillie in 2011, just before I began facilitating my very first dream circle in Los Angeles. At the time, I was collaborating with a life coach on a burgeoning YouTube channel where online guests would share a dream, I would offer an interpretation, and my partner would chime in with coaching guidance based on the conversation that would ensue. One time when we needed a last-minute replacement guest, we found a woman named Lillie, who lived nearby, had the availability that day, and swooped in to save the day's recording. I had just started my very first dream circle and was looking for a permanent home for that monthly gathering. Lillie was excited to offer her home, and we began holding our monthly gatherings at her place.

Within two years, we outgrew her living room and had to move to more substantial quarters, but because of this monthly contact, Lillie had the opportunity to dive into her dreamwork in a way that was, ultimately, life-changing for her.

Let's backtrack to Lillie before she came in contact with my work. "I don't recall ever not lucid dreaming" is how she put it. It was not the case with every single dream, of course, but the experience had been lifelong by the time we started working together in the early 2010s. What transpired for Lillie by working with me was that she now had language for the organic experience that had always been part of her dreaming. This was a ripe time in her life for a deeper experience of self-investigation through dreamwork. My work broke the dreaming experience down for her in her waking-life understanding of how her dreams were speaking to her, generating for her a structure for considering what certain dream images might be representing. What was extraordinary about this is that this waking-life information, and the distinctions about dreaming that she was learning during the day, began to show up in her lucid dreams.

There are certain basic concepts in dream interpretation that are rooted in universal principles. For example, water is evidence of emotional conflict being examined. Dreams of homes of any sort are likely expressing how a dreamer is feeling about their sense of self at the time of the dream. All people in dreams represent aspects of the self, but famous people reflect higher, aspirational energies around elements of our humanity. These constructs spoke to Lillie very directly, and it was easy for her to incorporate this way of working with dreams into her already significant experience of self-investigation. But when these ideas about interpretation started to show up as lucid thoughts within her dream state, I knew I was seeing something pretty unusual play out. Here is how Lillie described this to me when I interviewed her for this book.

> You broke it down for me, and then I realized that the more language I had for understanding my dreams when I was awake, the more that knowledge started showing up in my dream experiences. So I found that in my dreams I was starting to have conversations with myself about what something might mean. The president at the time was Clinton, and I recall a dream about him where I was like, "Oh, I'm dreaming about President Clinton, so that's my higher self and my masculine energy," and I would be interpreting the dream while it was happening. Or, "I'm going downstairs, so I must be visiting the lower depths of my unconscious." Or, "Muddy water—oh gosh, that's all these cloudy emotions I'm feeling."

Not all experiences of dream lucidity are quite as direct and obvious as Lillie's, but plenty of people have reported lucid experiences where a dream is playing out while simultaneously offering an interpretation of what the dream is revealing. The next example is an experience that is similar to that of the lucid interpreter, where the dreamer received some guidance about the meaning of the dream in the context of the dream itself. Lori, a woman in her mid-forties who was, at the time, in the process of training to become a life coach with a Jungian bent, described the dream like this.

I am pregnant in the dream, and when I notice that I am pregnant, my belly begins to grow very suddenly and very fast. The baby is sitting very high on my belly, so I know it's a boy. I am aware that there is this presence in the dream, like a narrator. It is not me, but it is also not clear who this person is. I feel their presence in the dream as a kind of commentator. My feelings in the dream are fearful. I'm forty-three, and this could be dangerous. Will this baby be safe? Before I know it, my belly has swollen completely, and the baby, indeed a boy, just easily falls out of me, and the whole thing is graceful and easy. This is when the narrator says to me, "You see? This is how easy it can be." I know in the dream this voice is talking about my coaching business and the things I have to create. It is not quite that I know I am dreaming, but I am absolutely aware that in the dream I am being shown something important about my fears.

Indeed, by the time Lori had this dream experience, she was already oriented to trusting her dreams, and understood the importance of them. Not only did the lucidity of this dream in particular deepen her personal commitment to working with her dreams in this way generally, but the content of the dream itself was tremendously important with regard to Lori's path through life.

Not all lucid dream experiences are powerful and transformative. There is a fascinating lucid dream state that I have personally experienced several times in my life and that I have heard echoed enough times from others to put this dream structure on the list of potential ways we can become lucid in the dream state. Here is how one dreamer described their experience to me.

> I am in a place where there is just movement. I am connected to my sense of my body, though it is a dream, so it's less about my body and more about what I am seeing. And what I am seeing is movement. Like I'm in a kind of amusement park ride that just moves forward past places with objects and all sorts of things to see, but I am moving, so it's not about stopping and exploring, but just following this flow. It's moving forward. And then I get lucid. I realize I am dreaming, and that sense is so intense. Then I get the idea that I can impact what I am experiencing, so I use my mind (my intention, I guess) to change the direction I am moving in. And when I think "right," the movement banks to the right. I can change it, and I start moving in that direction. It's almost like I head in the direction I'm looking, and if I change where I'm looking, that's where I move. And I'm fully in control of this, and it's pretty exciting. But that's all, and then I wake up.

This reminds me of a dream experience that I've had a number of times in my life. The feeling of lucid awareness is complete, and I indeed have a sense of control and an ability to direct what is happening, but not with any sort of creative sophistication. Hearing this story from another dreamer was one of the ways I was able to understand this phenomenon as something universal, and then I began to hear this same experience described by other dreamers. While this particular version of lucid dreaming does not lend itself to replication, or attempting to stimulate the experience to occur, having this experience is one of the indications that your dreamworld is opening up and bleeding into your conscious awareness. This can generate a profound sense of connection to greater energetic experiences of being alive and human.

Lucid Dreaming Can Be Cultivated

The idea that people can increase the likelihood of generating more lucid dreaming has spawned a not-unsubstantial industry of books, classes, and workshops devoted to helping people have more vibrant experiences of this phenomenon. A number of different techniques are being taught to increase the likelihood of generating lucid dreaming. However, there is one technique that has been ubiquitous in the many decades that I have been exploring all things dreaming, which is in order to trigger a lucid experience while sleeping, the dreamer is encouraged to look at their hands throughout the day in their waking life.

The instruction is simple. Hold your two hands up in front of your face and look at them, and do this multiple times a day. The expectation is that eventually the image of your hands in front of your face will show up in a dream. Because so much waking-life attention has been put into cultivating this image, the promise is that when you do indeed see your hands in your dreams, a conscious thought will pop up in the dreaming state. The theory is that you will instantly understand that you are dreaming, and this implanted suggestion of the expectation of this image is what triggers this lucidity.

Let's take a look at why this technique might actually be a perfect way to trigger a richer experience of lucid dreaming. In order to understand this, we have to dive into one of the aspects of REM sleep and dreaming as it relates to clearing the enormous amount of data we receive each day. The brain works a lot like a computer, at least at our current level of understanding of how it functions. The brain is powered by electricity, and the impulses that occur at the level of a single brain cell are a series of single nerves in the brain sending little bursts of electricity, one to another. You look at the muffin you are about to eat, and your eyes see the object and register what it is. Your sense of smell kicks in as you bring the tasty morsel toward your mouth. The taste of muffins will explode into the experience, and memories of past muffins will flood your brain.

What I just described probably takes about two seconds of time to play out. Inside of that incredibly brief moment, millions of nerve cells are sending out little bursts of energy to the cells next to them, and after a few million of these connections are made, the brain registers: incoming muffin. Now multiply that exponentially, considering every single thing you take in during the day. While this, of course, applies to what you are aware of, understand that your brain is busy all day, furiously filling in gaps and adjusting perceptions to offer you a clear-enough glimpse of the world around you to function—and not bump into the furniture too often. By the time you head to bed at the end of the day, your brain is at full capacity for what it can turn into cogent, accurate perceptions. If you didn't clean and clear out the cache of your brain, you would not function effectively, just like how your computer will slow down if there is too much processing is going on and a clearing-out needs to take place. If you reboot your computer, the operating system will run smoothly again, and this is sort of what happens when we sleep.

It is during REM sleep that we review everything we have experienced during the day as a process of clearing out the brain's resources for functioning. Although this happens at the quantum level, the process works something like this. Remember that muffin? Well, so does your brain, only it is not a form made out of flour, eggs, and sugar, but a series of pathways that the brain has carved out with electricity, and now that muffin exists in your consciousness as a function of an uncountable number of neurons that have created a chain in the brain that we call a neural pathway. During REM sleep, one of the things your brain is busy doing is retriggering that pathway we are calling "muffin." The brain then decides to keep or pass. Anything important becomes part of our short-term memory, and all the rest falls into the abyss of that which remains unconscious. We wake up the next day remembering that we ate a muffin yesterday morning, but that's about it.

Now multiply this process exponentially and you have some idea of just how crazy busy the brain is during REM sleep, and because part of the brain is busy reviewing all the data from the day, it is very common for dream experiences to include things that actually happened during the day. In this way, you can think of memory formation and the bizarre images of dream narratives to be separate functions in the brain. Somewhere way beyond our current level of understanding, the two experiences combine. So if you have been looking at your hands every day often, and do this consistently, eventually it is likely that in the dream state, that part of your brain that is producing dream images will collide with the part of your brain that is reviewing the day's experiences, and one night, there it will be: your hands in front of your face.

The promise is that once you have had this initiatory experience of creating a deliberate bleed from your conscious waking life into your dream landscape, you will have popped the barrier, and more lucid experiences are likely to follow. As with anything we wish to cultivate, time, experience, and repetition are key. There are many people who are simply wired to have lucid dream experiences for reasons we do not yet understand from a scientific perspective. Most people are not oriented this way. If you are someone who has little or no organic experience with lucidity in dreams, this approach is probably your best entry to expanding what is possible for you to enter your dreams in a more conscious way.

In my travels, I stumbled upon an approach to developing and cultivating a lucid dream experience that was reported to me by a client who had a pretty powerful experience of achieving the intended result. The focus in this approach starts with something that I think is imperative when seeking to have a greater bleed between the conscious mind and unconscious spaces, and that is meditation. Without some sort of meditative discipline, most people's minds are so chaotic that it can be nearly impossible to generate enough quietness in the mental landscape for such subtle energetic phenomena to occur. We start with the understanding that any exploration of higher consciousness needs to be supported by the discipline of meditation as a daily practice.

Our sleep stages support this notion in that we start the process of sleep with an alert mind, where if we were measuring the electrical impulses of brain waves, we would see wildly chaotic brain wave activity that is concomitant with wakefulness. As we drop into the first three stages of sleep, with each stage we enter successfully, that chaotic and seemingly random brainwave activity begins to synchronize, and by the time we get to the third stage of sleep, those waves are moving in a way that is no longer random and disorganized, but rather in a kind of flow. This is exactly what the discipline of meditation can generate. So if you want to have powerful experiences of energetic phenomena of any kind, but especially those related to sleep and lucid dreaming, *there needs to be a certain setup in the brain of receptivity,* and daily meditation is the most direct way of increasing this potential.

Setting an Intention Is Key

The next focus is all about intention, the most powerful tool we have as human beings. The idea that we can long for things that do not exist and use our focused thoughts to manifest in the world something that is not yet in form is the miracle of human consciousness. When we utilize this tool, we can create more than we can imagine. This particular approach to generating a lucid dream experience includes flooding the waking mind with the specific dream experience we want to generate. Every day, multiple times a day, you are encouraged to stop what you are doing, take a moment to turn within, and state, and then restate, your desired intention to encourage a lucid dream to rise up.

Here's the important thing: the desire has to be strong for an intention to take hold. With any manifestation, we must start with an idea, a thought, like a seed we plant that contains all the potential of the thing desired. Then it is the emotional body that provides the sustenance, like water and nutrients, to help encourage that seed to crack open and germinate. The idea itself is the kernel of this experience, but it is the ability to feel excited about the possibility that is the real key to having an intention turn into form. One may have a strong desire to have a lucid dream experience, but that is not quite powerful enough and is much too general for the psyche to grab a hold of.

This particular approach to lucid dreaming has a very specific structure. Choose someone famous, someone who has or had a large share of universal awareness, and ask them to come into your dream state for an interview. That way, the desire to interview this person in the dream state will tap into a more powerful sense of passion in your psyche. Their celebrity status alone is enough to trigger you with the high-stakes excitement of connecting to the specific person in question. Asking for just anyone to come into a dream interview and bring a sense of lucidity might be powerful for a person seeking a numinous experience in their dreams. But by choosing an individual who excites a deep passion in you, the process lights up a much deeper impulse in your unconscious that will have more creative mojo, increasing the likelihood of the desired outcome. The higher the stakes, the more likely you are to be successful.

A dreamer in one of my classes chose his obsession: Marilyn Monroe. He deepened his meditative practice for the six weeks of the course I was teaching. He diligently worked on his intention by writing it down frequently, adding the intention to his meditation experiences, and periodically quieting his thoughts during the day and focusing on his desire: "Marilyn Monroe, please come to me in my dream so that I can interview you." He was passionate about this, and his consistent and dogged approach paid off. One evening while sleeping, he fell into a dream and found himself in a kind of empty space. He was sitting in a chair, with an empty chair in front of him. After a time, Marilyn Monroe appeared, sat down in the other chair, and declared, "I'm ready for my interview." What followed felt to him very much like a waking-life experience, and the memory of the dream lives inside him like an actual experience, as if he actually did meet his idol in real time.

I have had two lucid dreams in my life that rank among the top, most numinous experiences I have ever had. This was not the kind of dreamlike experience where a conscious thought entered in and made me aware that I was in fact dreaming. The first of these took place in the living room of the apartment I was living in at the time. I was wide awake, in the middle of the day, just relaxing on my couch. It was then that I realized I was dreaming, but I was not in a dream state; I was absolutely fully and completely awake in my life, in the present day. I was as awake in that moment as I am now, writing this paragraph in my current office. I was asleep, and was aware that I was not only asleep, but asleep in the other room. It was an uncanny experience, and the sensation of that experience is beyond my ability to convey in words. Imagine if you were sitting reading this book, fully in your body, wide awake. Now add the realization that you were dreaming, and you knew it was a dream, and you will get some sense of the lucidity of this dream.

Several years later, I had another lucid dreaming experience. This dream featured a picnic table in an outdoor park–like setting. I was as wide awake as can be, but instead of the crisp, sharp sunlight of midday, there was a sepia haze over everything, which was quite remarkable. The feeling in my body was one of conscious alertness, but the quality of the light told me immediately that I was not in the three-dimensional world—though, again, I was as awake in that moment as I am now, writing these words. There were five other people sitting at the picnic table. My memory tells me that they were all men, but I may be adding that dimension to my memory. I got my bearings, looked around, and approached the table. I was standing next to the table where these five men were seated, and I addressed them all: "You understand that we're all dreaming this, right?" My question was met with enthusiastic agreement, and I woke with the absolute conviction that there were six human beings connecting in the dream state, having a lucid dream of sitting at a picnic table, in a lovely park, on a beautiful sunny day.

In my journey as an expert in dreams and dream interpretation, I have spoken to thousands of people about their dreaming, and a handful of them are natural lucid dreamers. Without effort or specific focus, these individuals have regularly occurring experiences of lucidity on all sorts of levels. Though I have devoted my life to exploring this human experience, I am not such a person, which has left me feeling a bit of envy at times. I personally have never been drawn to explore this phenomenon more diligently with the intention of increasing the frequency of lucid dreaming. That said, my two very powerful personal examples of this type of dreaming have left me with the absolute certainty that this potential of the human psyche to allow conscious awareness to move into places that are absolutely the realm of the unconscious is a *bona fide* phenomenon. It not only is natural and organic, but also can be nurtured, cultivated, and expanded.

There are a handful of other lucid dreaming techniques that can be found in books about the subject and have been offered by teachers over the years. One rather onerous-sounding process is focused on increasing the conscious awareness of that liminal space between sleeping and waking, when dream material is most actively available to the conscious mind in the process of waking up. The premise involves purposely waking yourself up during the night to take advantage of this state, which, by virtue of being in the middle of the sleep process, can open the dreamer up to the powerful in-between state. When we are done with sleep in the morning and the brain does not require another dip into REM sleep for restorative purposes, we rouse and are unlikely to fall back asleep. We move in and out of at least four, sometimes five, REM cycles throughout the night, each one getting longer and longer as the sleep progresses.

If you set your alarm for about four hours into sleep, you are likely to wake up after your second REM cycle. By virtue of coming into wakefulness right after dreaming, the process of writing your dreams down activates the unconscious-conscious bridge that exists in that liminal state between sleeping and waking. You then are to set your alarm for ninety minutes later, which is about the time for your next REM cycle, and are instructed to repeat the process every hour and a half until it is time for you to wake and begin your day. The principle behind this technique is pretty clear. By blurring the boundary between the sleeping consciousness and wakefulness, by rousing yourself enough to write your dreams down but not quite enough to snap your conscious awareness into full attention, you are strengthening that enormous energetic muscle. Your mind will, over time, become more accustomed to staying in that in-between state, and taking that slight bit of conscious awareness back into the state of sleeping. That bit of conscious awareness is more likely to show up in dreaming.

Here is a spin on the "looking at your hands" technique to induce lucid dreaming that also seeks to attach a thread of awareness to an action that occurs in waking life and then translate the awareness of that action into the sleep state. Dreamer Joni shared this experience with me about working with a technique she learned in a book about lucid dreaming by author Robert Waggoner called, simply, *Lucid Dreaming*. Among the many tips presented in this book, the one that worked the best for Joni was to develop the habit of holding her nose with her mouth closed several times during the day to confirm that she was awake. This works because cutting off the breath sparks the brain into activation, and the panic that ensues will cause anyone to respond to the blocking of the breath as a powerful instinct that all humans can identify with. It makes sense to use this particular physical intervention since the laws of physics do not apply to the dreaming landscape. Joni employed this technique for a few weeks and was excited about the result it generated.

> The short version of the dream is I was with a group of five or six people I am close to and we were sitting on couches, with a coffee table in the middle. I believed I was dreaming, so I plugged my nose with my mouth closed and continued to "breathe." I got really excited and said to everyone, "Hey, we're all in a dream together!" and asked them to plug their noses to prove it. A couple of the people could still breathe and got excited with me. The others could not breathe and looked at me like I was crazy.

As I was researching this book and dug into the different experiences of lucid dreaming that people have had, there was a theme that rose up involving interaction with powerful teachers and the potential for certain human beings with a high vibration to be able to generate energetic phenomena in those gathered around them. We have the word *guru* to describe such people operating at a very high level, but this sort of mastery can be embodied by many people who turn toward a spiritual path as teachers. One such experience was relayed to me by Jim, a man in his early fifties who had spent much of his adult lifetime in spiritual exploration. Lucid dreaming was a personal goal, and his many years of investigation through books, videos, and even working with binaural beats had yielded no real results.

Jim knew of a Buddhist teaching tract where, at the end of a three-year course of study, an initiation took place into a higher level of conscious awareness that was supposed to include lucid dreaming, Jim's personal holy grail. In the way that life often delivers us to interesting places, Jim stumbled upon a course near where he lived being taught by a lama who was also a Buddhist priest at a major American university. Synchronicities lined up, and Jim found himself studying with this man in a small community of about thirty people who all shared the desire to have experiences of lucid dreaming.

However, there was something unexpected in this course, where the lama teaching it announced that the students were welcome to be initiated into Buddhism through a ritual that included coming forward and allowing the lama to cut the initiate's hair. While no one else in the class stepped up for this process, our dreamer did. His hair was cut, and it was announced that he was now officially a Buddhist.

What happened next was fascinating. During the course, there was a program taught to the students where each night certain prayers were to be said and visualizations focused on. Jim was doing these things with great focus during the course, but once he received his initiation through this grooming ritual, he had a very vivid dream where, in the dream state, he had the unmistakable and lucid sense that the lama was energetically working with him. When he went to class the next morning, indeed the teacher arrived at class with a kind of announcement, and said, "A few of you were right there. All you need to do is open up and let it happen." This confirmed Jim's nighttime experience, and he continued to work on the rituals and was able to generate more glimpses into this powerful bleed between waking life and dreaming. While this experience didn't last beyond the course for Jim, the process helped deepen his ongoing commitment to immersing himself in his spiritual path, and allowing the dream state to be a big part of that experience.

Dreaming on Demand

One aspect of lucid dreaming includes the ability to come out of a dream and move into some level of wakefulness and then return to the same dream on demand. Part of the experience of cultivating lucid dreaming connects to how you treat the experience of simply being in bed when you move through moments of rousing throughout the night. This is where your daytime meditation practice will come in very handy. The skills that are cultivated in waking-life meditation can be put to use in these liminal spaces in between dreaming to increase the likelihood of becoming lucid in the dream state. Returning to a dream in an intentional way becomes far easier when you have a strong muscle for moving into trance states while awake.

In the many interviews I did for this book, Elise was the dreamer whose ability to generate powerful states of trance reflected my own. She described a process of working in her mind's eye using breath and toning techniques to open up her instrument to the energy that organically flows through us all. Meditation has the effect of synchronizing brain waves that are characteristically chaotic and seemingly random. A person with a diligent meditation practice executed over time trains their brain to respond to this inner discipline. The net resulting change in brain wave patterns matches what the brain is doing organically in the first few stages of sleep.

Elise will rouse in the middle of the night, just as we all do. And while she doesn't set an alarm to wake up this way, as suggested earlier in this chapter, what she does in those moments has allowed her to have many lucid dream experiences, including returning to a dream she had been having just before waking up. She has woken up in this state and been so lucid at times that she felt like she was awake when she was still actually asleep and dreaming. There are many journals in which she has logged these semiconscious, semi-lucid experiences in which she feels like she has received information from sources outside of herself. In fact, the feeling of this experience is so like waking, even if she is still asleep, that she has developed the habit of reaching over to touch her dog, who sleeps next to her. If she makes actual contact with her dog, then she knows she is awake. If not, then she allows the semi-lucid experience to take over.

When asked about her history with this experience, Elise shared with me that it started in childhood because of some guidance offered by her mother. As a child, Elise had frequent nightmares. She shared these terrifying dreams with her mother, who offered some guidance to this five-year-old girl that, in my experience, is rare for a parent to say to a child about such dreaming experiences. Most parents will instinctively attempt to comfort a frightened child by minimizing the experience, saying things like, "It's just a dream." This negates the powerful and very real experience that the child is having internally. Having a parent dismiss such an experience is confusing and sets up a disconnect between the child and their own internal landscape. Elise's mother lovingly suggested that Elise turn around in any dream and look at whoever or whatever was chasing her, and suggested that by doing so, they would disappear. Elise was only four or five years old at the time, but the information took, and this was the start of a lifelong relationship with dreaming experiences that also featured prominently in Elise's journey of spiritual awakening.

My last example of lucid dreaming is a story that combines so many different types of mystical experiences that it could fit in other chapters of this book as well. It also echoes what we learned from Elise and her mom's good advice. There is a gentleman named Eli whose dream experiences found their way into several of this book's chapters, and Elise's story was fresh in my mind the first time I sat down with Eli to cull his vast experience of mystical dreams and see what I might share in these pages. At the time of this writing, Eli was a man in his seventies who, like me, began to have powerful and vivid dreams as early as three years old. Because of Eli's organic relationship to dreaming as a young boy, once he entered adulthood, he began a pretty comprehensive dive into all things spiritual. What I am about to share with you involves not only lucid dreaming, but also connections to past lives and the profound way that all things are deeply connected.

Early in his adult life, Eli found himself connecting to a spiritual community whose practices included a meditative process that was designed to encourage lucid dreams. The technique he learned included lying in bed for at least three nights in a row. The practitioners were encouraged to center in their body and lie still on their back, with their hands lying gently on their thighs, in a posture of devout stillness. There was even a suggested direction they were to lie in to maximize this psyche-body connection they were charged with generating. Then a mantra was added, to be said over and over again as sleep rose up: "Tonight I am

going to become conscious and awake and aware in my dream."
This practice was that simple, and like most such practices, the
magic was in discipline and repetition.

This experience of Eli's took place in his early twenties, but
the powerful lucid dream he had involved a recurring dream
that had begun when he was just three years old. Every few
months starting at this young age, Eli had a recurring nightmare
in which a man in a Nazi uniform was chasing him through his
house with a knife. Eli understood that his three-year-old self
could not possibly have recognized such a uniform as belonging
specifically to a person in the Nazi party, but as he got older and
learned more about the world, it became clearer to him that
this recurring dream avatar was a German soldier.

By the time Eli took this class in his mid-twenties, he had had
this particular dream dozens of times. The dream was essentially the same, though the house he found himself in would
shift if his family moved to a different domicile. It was not surprising that during the time frame in which he was working on
this technique as part of this spiritual community, this chasing
dream returned.

The dream started as it always did, with the man chasing
Eli. The house in this particular version of the dream was the
one Eli lived in for about nine years of his childhood. After a bit
of the dream content played out, Eli did indeed become lucid
in the dream. He "woke up" in the dream state, took a very
deep breath, turned around to face his assailant, and out of his
mouth came the question, "Why are you chasing me?"

The Nazi replied, "There's a sealed-up doorway over here
and I'm trying to get into it and I can't get in. Could you help

me?" What Eli saw was indeed a door frame, but there appeared to be no actual door there. Upon closer inspection, he could see that the edges of the door were there, but they appeared to have been plastered over. The dream Nazi had been trying to scrape off the plaster, but had not been able to free the doorway from its plastered confines.

The Nazi then handed Eli the knife, which he took and used to scrape out all of the plaster. Thanks to his efforts, the door swung open. The door led to a small square room, about eight feet by eight feet, painted a very dark green. In the far-right corner, there was a little square of concrete, creating a small raised platform just above floor level. Perched on this shelf was a little bubbling pool of water, squirting water up out of it, like a fountain, but more organic than a human-made structure. On the left side of the room was a shelf on the wall, and on that shelf sat a skull. After assessing the scene for a moment, Eli turned back around to say to this man in the Nazi uniform, "Look what's here!" But the man was gone, and the dream ended.

Once Eli broke through the wall of lucidity, after two decades of having this dream on a regular basis, he never had the dream again, not ever. This is very curious, as if somehow the recurring dream signaled a conflict that Eli's soul was forcing him to face in the dream state. Like many conflict moments, it dissolved once the desired need was met. It was as if his soul needed him to see this connection, and the need dissipated as soon as the important information was understood and integrated.

There were some personal associations that Eli made at the time that he had the final Nazi dream. One was the peculiar dark green color of the room in the dream, which matched the color of the basement of one of the homes he grew up in on Long Island, New York. Another, much more vibrant connection Eli made was to the skull on the shelf, which came from a trip he had made to Israel, where he visited a monastery at Mount Sinai. On a tour of this very old monastery, Eli had visited a huge room that was filled with the bones of all of the monks who had ever lived there. Peculiarly, the bones were divided into piles. Large bones were grouped together, another place was reserved for the smaller bones, and there was yet a third pile where the skulls had been tossed. However, if a monk had enjoyed a particularly high status in life, such as achieving the status of an abbot, or had been famous or notable in some other fashion, his skull was placed on a shelf in this room instead.

Chapter Three

Shared Dreaming

The experience of shared dreams, where two people have the same dream at the same time, may sound like something right out of a movie. However, this can and does happen. Of course, it's possible that shared dreaming is much more common than we know, because unless people are habitually talking to others in their world about what they are dreaming about, how could they know if they are sharing dream space with them? I have spoken to thousands of people who do share their dreams with others, and have found, not surprisingly, that the people who share dream experiences also have a close personal relationship with each other in waking life.

Beyond the obvious case of close connections encouraging the potential for shared dreaming, shared high-stakes life events can increase this possibility as well. For example, it is not uncommon for couples who are pregnant to share dreaming experiences. Perhaps this is because of the heightened chemical intensity of pregnancy combined with the power of shared experiences between expectant mother and father in ways that are still a mystery. And, of course, this scenario increases the likelihood of even discovering that such a phenomenon is happening, because the parties involved are more likely to share the intimacy of their dream experiences with each other in conversation. Another common scenario that often elicits the same sort of evidence of shared dreaming is when someone is making their life transition and passing into death.

There are people with an advanced development of innate intuition, so one might expect such individuals to be more likely to have these experiences. We met Eli in the previous chapter on lucid dreaming, and he had some interesting experiences from decades ago when he was first getting onto his spiritual path. In the 1980s, he was also exploring his role as a teacher, and dreams and dreaming became a big part of his focus, given that his own personal experience of dreaming had been so vibrant from a very young age. He and a colleague decided to run an experiment. They created two groups of dreamers for a project that lasted an entire year. The two groups were a bit like a study group and a control group, where the expectation was that these groups would perform differently, as one group was made up of seasoned dreamers who all knew each other in a community that already existed, and the other was a group of people who were not only strangers, but also novices to this kind of work with dreams.

In the group of strangers, the assignment was to meet up in their dreams in the head of the Statue of Liberty, a simple and consistent image that this group, who all lived in New York City, would easily recognize if they were successful in sharing a dream locale with one another. The more seasoned group approached this experiment with slightly more sophistication, where the location might change from month to month. With both groups, they timed their experiment with the New Moon each month. Eli told me, "It was amazing how often both groups met up [in their dreams], not always in the designated locations, but sometimes somewhere else. I remember a month when most of the strangers found themselves on a horse ranch, which was something we'd never talked about. But very often they did find each other in the head of the Statue of Liberty."

It is interesting to me that it was the group of novice strangers that had more success during this year than the seasoned practitioners. The novices saw one another in their dreams such that they were able to describe the other people physically with amazing accuracy, even though they had never met in person. I think that Eli's experiment speaks to the untapped intuitive power of the dream state, and the fact that such things can be cultivated and expanded to increase intuition and have a greater sense of collective connection with all human beings through the dream state. While this was a cultivated experience, I have found lots of evidence that shared dreaming can and does happen, even to people who are not seeking it out.

Family Members Sharing Dreams

Family members have both the intimacy and the close proximity needed to easily find experiences of shared dreaming, and there is nothing quite like a high-stakes moment, such as the death of a family member, to provide the third ingredient of unusual energetic circumstances to stir up something interesting. I heard a story from dreamer Kate, who shared the following with me:

I was fourteen years old and my sister was thirteen when she and I had the same exact dream the night after our mother passed away. In the dream, my mother was hiding behind our bedroom door. I kept calling out to her to come out fully so that I could see her, but she refused to come out. Then I started to pester her some more, but she would only show half of her face and body while the rest was hidden behind the door. Her face was very serious, sad, and casted over with a shadow, so I began to get a little freaked-out. Then I woke up. At breakfast, I kept this to myself, but my sister said she had a dream with Mama and I told her, "Me too!" When I told her mine, she got really quiet and said "I had the same exact dream."

I have heard more than one version of this example, and partly because of the belief that intense connections in waking life can lead to this sort of shared dream experience. Additionally, if the idea of visitations from loved ones who have just passed away is something that is entertained by the surviving family members, it stands to reason that the mechanism that sparks such psychic and extrasensory experiences might very well be the mystery of dreaming. Death itself is a multidimensional experience, and so are dreams. In this way, an energetic connection between a recently deceased mother and both of her daughters in the same dream at the same time makes sense.

A dreamer in her early forties, Lori PK, had a dream of her mother dying on the same day that her daughter had a dream of her mother (Lori PK) dying.

So, in my dream, I was with my mom, we were outside, and we decided to get inside this area that looked like a big, huge hotel, mall—I couldn't figure out exactly, but like a collective place to rest and shop. And as we walked inside, instead of taking the stairs, my mom, she decided to, it's hard to say, so she thought she saw the stairs, but actually it was a big void like a cliff. And she thought the stairs were right there, and she went from that area and she fell and I could hear her neck breaking as she hit the ground. And there were people on the other side, so I was looking at the people's reaction, which was traumatized, and I could hear the noise of my mom falling from this big void. And I couldn't dare to look at her. But I reached, a little later, I reached my neck to see where she was and I couldn't see her physically. So, at the moment I was a little, like, scared and confused. Did she really die? Was she okay?

This is the moment when Lori PK woke up, feeling pretty shaken about the dream she had just had. While she was lying in bed, ruminating on what the dream might mean for her, her eleven-year-old daughter, with whom she was sharing a room at that time, woke up. The very first thing she said to her mother after opening her eyes was, "Mom, I just had a dream and you died in my dream." Needless to say, this intrigued our dreamer, so mother asked daughter to share the dream with her, even taking notes. This is what Lori PK described about her daughter's dream.

In her dream, she (Lori PK's daughter) was walking back from my neighbor's house, where her best friend lived. She opens the front door and comes into the house, and goes right into my office, where I normally sit and at my computer. I call this my studio. She opens the door to my studio and she sees a version of me sitting at my desk, but she realizes right away that it's not a real person, it's not her real mom. It's someone else, like a virtual image, and it tells her, "Your mom just got killed by the cat." She looks, and she realizes that I was killed because she saw a puddle of blood on the floor. She didn't see my body, but she knew that I had been killed.

Because Lori PK was no stranger to dreamwork, she was able to interact with her daughter in a manner that did not dismiss this experience as "just a dream." After her daughter shared the dream, Lori PK took notes and asked her daughter to share her feelings, which included being confused and "weirded out." Both mother and daughter benefited from this interaction in ways that Lori PK was clear about. It will be interesting for her to see how her daughter grows to appreciate what can happen in the unseen realms.

The next example I present to you is a story that I came across in my research for this book about a shared dream experience that was also connected to a visitation dream. I decided to present it here because the beauty of this experience is most apparent in the fact that there was a shared dream experience between mother and son, even though the experience that the mother had was related to a simple but powerful visitation dream that happened the very first night that her mother passed.

It is possible for a visitation dream to feature auditory phenomena as opposed to visual. Mary Lynn comes from a very large and very close Catholic family, with a strong sense of matriarchal structure. As is often the case with such dynamics, the mother was the strong central hub of this large clan. Mary

Lynn's mother died quite suddenly of a heart attack, sending the entire family into an unexpected crisis of grief. The first night after she passed, Mary Lynn went to sleep with the perseverating thought of, "How will our family survive without Mom?" In her dreams later that night, Mary Lynn had the very clear experience of hearing her mother's voice in response. She heard, "Don't worry. Everything is going to be okay."

Now, this sort of visitation dream was not foreign to Mary Lynn. She reports having been visited before by relatives who had passed. And always, those dreams were auditory in nature, so Mary Lynn trusted the experience she'd had when she woke up the next morning. As she started her day in the kitchen making breakfast, her then-thirteen-year-old son walked into the kitchen and said, "Mom, Grandma came to me last night. She said, 'Don't worry. Everything is going to be okay.'" They weren't similar words; they were the exact same words.

This was a profound moment for Mary Lynn in that it was undeniable to her that indeed, as irrational as it may have felt, her mother's spirit was present and expressing herself to the family in the dream state. I love everything about what this tells us about the instability of what we call reality. Somehow this little story illustrates perfectly our notion of what is real life and what is the dreamworld. We trust the three-dimensional world of form to be, well, real, and the world we contact during sleep is the fantastic non-reality. From this story, it is possible to conclude that the truer experience of consciousness itself is not the waking life, but what happens in dreams.

Another mother and daughter I spoke to had a shared dream experience where there was a bit of a handoff. The mother had the first part of the dream, but the completion of that same narrative was experienced by the daughter that same evening. This happened when the daughter was in her mid-twenties and our dreamer, Joni, was in her mid-fifties, and the adult daughter was living at home. As many of these conversations take place in the kitchen, that morning Joanie had the impulse to tell her daughter about a dream she had had, in an uncharacteristic sharing of dreams, which was just not standard conversation in that household.

"I don't even know why I told her this dream," Joanie told me, "because it was so seemingly insignificant, but I said, 'Hey, you were in one of my dreams last night. We were here in the kitchen and we decided that we wanted to make pancakes.'" Her dream was of the beginning of the process of making pancakes, cracking eggs, measuring flour, and mixing the batter. Joni's daughter was astonished as she told her mother what she had dreamt about the night before: "I had a dream last night that we were in the kitchen with the bowl of pancake batter, and so we heated the pan, made the pancakes, sat down, and ate them." This shared dream was like a two-act handoff, where the mother started the preparation of the meal in the first act and the daughter took up the part of making and eating the pancakes in the second act.

Clearly, a marital and/or family connection can be a good indicator that shared dreaming is a potential. Ellie, a woman in her fifties whom I have worked with extensively over the years, has a rich history of dreaming experiences, including a few that fall into this category of shared dreams. The first shared dream she reported happened in her early thirties, when she was first married to her husband and living in Paris. This was a rich moment for her spiritual sensibilities, because she felt deep energetic connections to Paris in a way that felt like she had past-life connections with this city, and this was the period in her life when her spiritual path began in earnest. Since her husband never shared his dreams with her, it was uncharacteristic of him to wake up one morning very captivated by a dream he'd had, with an accompanying need to share it.

He was disturbed by the dream, and even during the telling of it to his wife as they lay together in bed, he held his head and kept his eyes closed. "I had this dream that I was a slave in this dungeon. I was an African man, and I was a slave in chains, and it was just horrible," he said with some deep agitation.

Ellie was astonished, because not only was this sharing completely out of character for her husband, but she had also had a shockingly similar dream that same night, and told him, "I can't believe it! I had a very similar dream. I was in a dungeon and I was chained up."

Ellie's dream was very vivid, and in it she saw herself as a sort of Catherine Zeta-Jones type from movies she had seen. In the dream, she was the hot, sexy slave woman, while another slave, an African man, came in and ripped off the chains and rescued her. As they went off together in the dream, Ellie reports that she knew they were being punished for having had some sort of illicit affair. Given that this was a time in her life when her spiritual sensibilities were opening up, she even took the risk of sharing with her husband that she felt like she was tapping into a past-life experience, and that he, her husband, was sharing that experience with her through the dream state.

Of course, he dismissed this as a coincidence that should be ignored. Ellie knew better, and her life has since brought her many such dream experiences.

The second time a shared dream happened in Ellie's life was seven years later. By then, Ellie and her husband had welcomed their first child, a daughter whom Ellie describes as intuitive and empathic. They woke up one morning, and in her four-year-old sweetness, the daughter said, "Oh Mama, I had the nicest dream that we were picking flowers together in a field." Now this might have been just another dream of many described by this young girl, only Ellie had had a vivid dream that same night of being in a beautiful field of flowers, picking them with her daughter.

Ellie's third experience of shared dreaming was not quite as sweet, and was accompanied by a rather disturbing life event. In 2016, an armed shooter entered the Pulse nightclub in Orlando, Florida, and shot and killed multiple people in a terrifying attack. By then, Ellie had fully developed her intuition and the many energetic gifts she was blessed to explore, so this shared dream experience is also an example of a precognitive dream, where a dreamer connects to world events through the dream space. In Ellie's dream, and much like what was described later by survivors of the Pulse massacre, there was a terrorist with a gun running around the environment trying to shoot Ellie and her friends and family. The dream was so disturbing that it woke her up, and she immediately got out of bed and went to the bathroom to perform that thing that you think only happens in movies, until you yourself are moved to splash cold water on your face to snap yourself out of some agitated state.

A bit later, when Ellie's husband woke up, he once again described a dream in a way that was consistent with his usual limited sense of the value of dreams. "I had the worst dream. It was like there was a shooting," he explained. While he didn't offer many details, the essence of both their dreams was the same. By now, Ellie had had many precognitive dreams involving close relatives and things that might be happening with them. However, it wasn't until she turned on the news that day that she understood immediately that both she and her husband had been tapping into the events that took place overnight three thousand miles away on the other side of the United States. At the time, Ellie was working with a spiritual enterprise coach, a man who also happens to be gay. When she reached out to him later that day, she was not really surprised that he, too, had had a dream the night before of being inside a cage in a very crowded venue. In the dream, he made many attempts to free himself from the cage, but was unable to, and after a while he could hear gunshots exploding over and over.

Shared Dreams Between Friends

Cathy is a dreamer who shared with me how she attempted to have a shared dream with a friend she felt very connected to in an energetic way. It was actually the friend's idea for the two of them to see if their waking-life connection might help them meet up in the dream space. The intention was set, and it involved something that ultimately connected them in waking life. The friend was from a coastal town, where proximity to the ocean reflected a way of life. Cathy was doing research for a book she was writing that took place in that area, so the location and activity of digging for clams made sense as a shared intention.

Cathy and her friend did indeed meet up that night in their dreams. There was no clam digging, as they had intended. The dream just had them sitting on a couch together. Cathy shared with me that she was not entirely sure that this experience hadn't been generated out of the power of suggestion, as opposed to being a genuine multidimensional experience involving them both. The deeper sense that she had, with which I concurred, was that their two souls did in fact meet up in dreams, and that this is something that happens and can be cultivated.

Lori (same name but different person from the Lori PK earlier in this chapter) is a woman in her fifties who has a close friend with whom she had a shared dream experience. Lori is a professional psychic, so she is naturally someone who is no stranger to energetic phenomena, though prior to this shared dream, she had never had such an experience through the dream state. Though she describes herself as someone who regularly has dreams that she remembers, most of her dreams have a floating-like sensation and feature the usual chaotic narratives that most people describe. She reports being only very occasionally lucid in the dream state, and she rarely has any nighttime experiences that are off the beaten path of her typical dreamscapes that she recognizes as her standard dreaming style.

However, one night, Lori had a dream experience that she described in this way:

I walked into an actual place I've gone to in my life, like a secondhand store with furniture, clothing, or whatever. I walked in and I had sold something, or had something to do with the counter, so I walked up to the counter. I looked over to the furniture area and there was a person, seemed like a woman but I wasn't sure. Long dark hair and this face that was just beautiful. And when I say that, it was more of a vibe; it wasn't like the person was a fashion model, but I had a strong felt sense of real beauty. They looked back at me and my heart just swelled, and I thought, "Oh my god, that's my person! What's happening?"

But I had to get this task done. I got to the counter, and I kept looking over, and there was just no question that this person and I were just, it had taken this long and, just, "There you are, and whoa, I can't wait to see what this is all about, but I got to do this stupid paperwork." So, I was doing that, and they sent me into another room and I thought, "I can't go into another room. I have to stay in this room, near her." Another woman walked up to her, and I thought at first, "Oh of course she has a partner." But I was really clear that no, it was me. I was her person, and she was mine. She looked at me as she passed by and walked away, and I was like, "No, no, no," thinking about not letting her walk away, and then I woke up.

The next day, Lori received a phone call from a friend, someone who was also actually an ex-girlfriend. They had remained close friends years after their romantic connection ended. Lori describes her friend's dreaming experience as rather pedestrian and not at all mystical. In fact, most of the friend's dreams seem to reflect waking-life events pretty directly, with storylines that are much like what happens during the day. However, this particular morning was an exception, and Lori reports that during the phone call, her friend described her dream like this:

> I had the weirdest dream that I found your person, but they were in my dream. I saw your person, but it was terrible because I went into this party or building with rooms, and there were all these people. I saw her sitting on this couch. She had long dark hair, and I thought, "That's her, that's Lori's person. Where's Lori? I have to find her." I went room to room and I couldn't find you, but I knew you were in the building, and then I woke up.

Here's a fascinating story of an experience that was so powerful for the dreamer, who was in her mid-twenties at the time. She shared this with me many years later, and started the tale by explaining that the details of the experience were fuzzy in that way that happens with time passing. However, the felt sensations of that morning were ingrained in her body as a powerful day in the course of her life.

Our dreamer woke up on a beautiful spring morning feeling buoyant and happy, having had a restful night's sleep that included a really fun dream. The delightful sensations of that dream bled into her morning mood. She described going into the kitchen for her first cup of coffee, only to find her roommate already there, in a highly emotional state, quite agitated from her own nighttime experience. The roommate described having had a very disturbing dream that was so vivid, it left her in what she described as an awful emotional state.

The roommate described her dream to our dreamer, in which she was running all night through a landscape that was definitely recognizable to her as the desert in the Southwestern United States. The era was decidedly in the past, in what the dreamer defined as "cowboy times." She had to hide in holes that she found in the ground and caves that she came upon. There was a distinct sense that she was running from a group of men in this dream, and she perceived herself as dirty and disheveled. She also had the sense that she was a man in this dream, that she was herself but also someone else in the way that dreams can play out. She felt isolated, alone, and in danger, and the terror of the dream stayed with her long after waking.

Our dreamer never shared what her own experience had been that very same night. For reasons that our dreamer can't quite recall, she felt unable or unwilling to interrupt her friend's difficult morning with the dream that she'd had the night before. Perhaps she felt bad that her dream had left her in such a good and empowered mood, whereas her roommate's dream experience had been so terrifying. In our dreamer's dream, she was leading a posse of men in a setting that was a throwback to earlier times in the West of the US. The dream featured a narrative of her tracking a man and feeling powerful and thoroughly righteous in the manhunt she was clearly leading. Both of these dreams feel to me like they were tapping into past lives, and it's possible to imagine that these two twenty-something roommates have played this game of life before, only in the past as hunter and hunted.

Soul Mates and Relationship
Connections in Shared Dreams

There are connections that can be made in life that might be called a "soul mate" connection if we didn't have a need to reserve that term for a relationship that is romantic in nature. We can have many soul mates in life, and not all of them involve that sort of intimacy. As you have seen in this chapter, many such friendships feature connections that transcend the physical plane.

Katrina and her friend Katie have shared dreams since they first met as teenagers in the same Spanish class in high school. Their friendship has continued for twenty years, but the establishment of these two as lifelong friends actually started with a shared dream experience. In fact, at the time of the interview for this book, Katrina had lost her mother to cancer about six months prior, and the friend in question was moving through the experience of her mother having just been diagnosed with the same cancer. This was made even more interesting to me by virtue of the fact that the connection between these two friends began when they met back in high school with a shared dream about their fathers.

The pair met in a high school Spanish class where the teacher of that class was moving back to her home country of Ecuador and offered her students the opportunity to visit her abroad. Though Katrina and Katie were only casual classmate acquaintances at the end of the school year, they became friends through the planning and execution of this summer excursion. Interestingly, the malaria medication they were required to take upon entering the tropics also had a side effect of potentially increasing the intensity of dreaming. That first morning when they both woke up in Ecuador was revelatory.

The essence of the shared dream was that each of these dreamers found themselves in a similar setting where each of them was in a position to consider their father, only the fathers in their dreams were clearly not their real fathers. As they shared the details of each of their dreams, there were so many other shared images. Both dreams took place at a table, perhaps in a kitchen or dining room. Both young women saw papers on this table that, upon closer inspection, turned out to be their birth certificates. In each dream, the father's name was not on the forms; in fact, the essential narrative of each dream was the noticing of this omission. In our dreamer's dream, she even noted that in the dream state, inner images of her own father, swarthy, dark, and physically reflecting his Azorean Portuguese roots, were replaced by a startlingly Caucasian version of him, one that, at least physically, resembled her friend's dad. Both dreams featured a single setting and narrative, which set them apart from typical dreams and indicated that they were more likely to be reflecting some intuitive mystical connection that dreams provide. Both young women were impacted by this shared experience, and it solidified a lifelong connection.

Dreamer Katarina and her friend Kate do not see each other that often in their waking lives, but their entire friendship has been powerfully marked by dreams that connect them. In fact, dreaming of each other's parents has been a theme over the years. Katarina has had connections to Kate's experience of becoming a parent, including dreaming about Kate becoming pregnant after a traumatizing miscarriage. Katarina dreamed that Kate was going to become pregnant again and have a baby girl. In this dream, Katarina reports a felt sensation that it was the spirit of the miscarried baby that was connecting to her. Fairly soon after, Kate did indeed get pregnant again and carried that baby to term, and sure enough, it was a girl.

Dreamer Marybeth had an experience two decades before I began collecting stories for this book. Though she hadn't thought about how important this dream experience had been with regard to a pivotal relationship in her life, she reached out and shared a powerful story with me. In her fifties now, Marybeth reports that when she was twenty-four years old, she worked with a man named Tim, and after several months of working together, they developed a close, collegial relationship. Tim was older and married, and she was with someone else at the time. Though there wasn't an overtly romantic connection between them, the relationship was strong. He occasionally mentioned challenges with his marriage, but sharing the details of that were not part of their developing friendship.

Though Marybeth reports that dreaming of people she knows is a frequent experience for her, she had never dreamt of this man while their friendship was growing. At a certain point, Tim went on a trip that Marybeth knew to be some sort of spiritual pilgrimage. While he was gone, she had a very vivid dream that didn't feel to her at the time like it was a dream about him but rather was an energetic experience with him. She reports being in an almost indescribable space where there was so much light, it felt like she was floating in a beautiful but ungrounded space.

As I'm, like, floating, I meet Tim, and it's like it's a coincidence in the dream. "Oh, I'm surprised to see you here," I said. I think we had a conversation of some kind, which I don't remember now. But it was this feeling; what I remember most now is this feeling of floaty-ness and deep, deep, deep connection. Like I was surprised. "Oh wow, I love this person. I love you. Oh, but do I feel attracted? Ooh maybe ooh it's a little bit scary." But it was just, it felt really beautiful.

When Tim returned from his trip, Marybeth was excited to tell him about the dream because it felt important and seemed to have meaning with regard to their connection. What she didn't expect was his response. "Oh, I had a dream about you," he said. But then he added, "Be careful." This cryptic response led to a deeper conversation that took place in private not long after. Tim described having the exact same dream while he was away, of being in a light space, floating, but connected with her, and having an undeniable and almost overwhelming feeling of love.

That conversation led to Tim leaving his wife, Marybeth ending the relationship that she was in at the time, and the two exploring a passionate though short-lived romantic connection. This revolutionary change in their lives made sense at the time because of this shared dream. Eventually, Tim went back to his wife and Marybeth continued her life and didn't revisit this particular memory until she saw that I was working on this book and reached out to share her story with me.

Intimate, romantic relationships often allow for such intuitive connections to exist between two people. In one rather remarkable case, Ruth, a woman now in her fifties, reports that a significant relationship from earlier in her life first appeared in a dream. She dreamed of this man shortly before she met him in life, and in the dream he told her point blank that they were not going to be together. Though the dream content was more portentous than she wanted to admit, she began a relationship with him that lasted several years.

During their time together, there were several occurrences of shared dreams, especially when they slept in the same bed. Though there were many such experiences, the one that remains most clearly in Ruth's memory happened fairly early in their relationship. She dreamed that she was walking to meet a friend of hers and all sorts of crazy things began to appear, including monsters and other frightening dreamscape manifestations. She called out for her boyfriend, who indeed came to help her. Together, they battled the monsters made of light, and after defeating them in some rather scary combat, they went off to go meet their friend.

The next morning, Ruth's boyfriend told her about a dream that he'd had that same night. Without revealing the content of her own dream, Ruth listened as he told her of dreaming that she was in trouble. In his dream, he heard her calling desperately for him to go and help her, which he did. This sort of shared dream was a constant feature of their dreaming experience. Even their breakup occurred first in the dreamworld before manifesting in their waking life.

The Best Story of Shared Dreaming I Have Ever Heard

I will finish this chapter with the story of two friends who actually introduced me to the notion of shared dreaming in the first place. In all my years of working with dreams, I had never had a shared dream, nor had I even heard of the phenomenon until I met Blaire. Blaire is a deeply spiritual soul whom I had the pleasure of connecting with when I was working on *Dream Sight*, my very first book on dream interpretation. She became a bit of a muse for me, and her loving nurturance helped me face the daunting task of completing the manuscript for my first publishing deal. That connection continued, and I happened to have a chance meeting with Blaire and her best friend Amanda a number of years ago when Blaire brought Amanda to me for an astrological reading. That lovely afternoon, the pair shared with me a shared dream experience that they had recently experienced. Given that I was on the prowl for interesting dream material, I took that story and put it in the book I was working on at the time, my third, *Llewellyn's Little Book of Dreams*.

Blair and Amanda share a lifelong friendship, but to really tell the story, we must go back to Blair's childhood. Her family life provided a strange sort of dichotomy. On the one hand, she was exposed to spiritual principles very early on, and spent much of her adolescence studying the power of prayer and affirmation and was introduced to the notion that we create our own reality with how we are perceiving it. On the other hand, she experienced a level of abuse and neglect that was pretty nightmarish. By the time she was in her early thirties, she found that she no longer had access to her spiritual sensibility and had really fallen into a victim mentality because of everything that had happened to her. She says that she was mad at God, mad at the world.

Blair and Amanda went away for a long weekend at a beautiful cabin in the woods. They both needed a break. Amanda's father had just died, and Blair's was very sick. Now, Blair reports to have always had a gift for perceiving energy, and as lovely as this cabin was, there was something about it that felt dark and not quite right to her. Feeling silly about this, Blair said nothing to her friend, though the feeling wouldn't go away. At some point that weekend, the two decided to curl up for a nap together. Privately, Blair felt relieved that Amanda was willing to cuddle together, because that feeling had persisted, and Blair did not really want to sleep by herself. After sleeping for forty-five minutes, they both woke up screaming and shaking.

As it turns out, both women had been dreaming about almost the same thing. Both dreamt that something terrible and dangerous was coming to get them. For Amanda, it was two men. In Blair's dream, it was much more energetic, like a menacing dark force. Amanda saw the heads of baby dolls, and Blair saw actual murdered babies. Though the details were different, the feelings they described to each other seemed exactly the same. Amanda then revealed that had been having the same negative feelings about the cabin, which she felt a bit silly about it, so she chose to stay silent. They both agreed that no matter what, it was time to go, so they packed their things and left immediately. Here's what Blair had to say.

> That experience was an absolute turnaround for me. I immediately began to face the childhood wounds that had been so trying to get my attention. I got back on to my spiritual path. And though the healing I needed took some time, I have arrived at a place in my life now where my faith is strong and I no longer see myself as a victim of the things perpetrated on me in my childhood. My friend and I never

did find out anything about that cabin in the woods, but I know that my life took an amazing and important turn that weekend, and nothing has ever been the same.

The story does not end there, and in a happy accident of synchronicity, when I was asking for dream experiences of a more mystical nature for this book, Blair was one of the people who responded. At the very moment that I was sending out emails, Blair and Amanda were at it again. Initially it was an innocuous little dream experience where the phone rang one morning and Amanda told Blair that she'd had an awful dream that her father, who was dead in waking life, was still alive, and actually had been for many years. The awful sensation of the dream seemed connected to the realization that he had been alive and on the planet all this time but Amanda had not been aware of it, and the news felt devastating. "That's outrageous," replied Blair. "I had a dream last night that my father was alive and I was delighted. I hadn't known he was there, but I was so delighted he was."

This experience was the one that Blair reached out to share with me at the time. My request for dream material had arrived in her inbox just as they had this shared dream of paternal death. At the time, the meaning of the experience that the two mused about seemed to deal more with the theme of father issues, but as this story winds to its stunning conclusion, we will see it was really a "two sides of the same coin" experience about the powerful and final separation that death engenders. This chapter of the story was also fueled by powerful, intuitive dreams.

It was a decades-long tradition that at least twice a year, Blair and Amanda would run away to the woods together and enjoy a retreat from urban life by going to a resort area in Southern California near Idyllwild. This trip started out like any other, marked by the usual sense of freedom and ease that comes with a slower pace and lots of outdoor space. Doors are left unlocked, and Blair often feels the most connected to what she calls her "army of light workers" in a manner that both Blair and Amanda are hip to. This trip was decidedly different. Each night Blair would wake up terrified that she had not locked the house. This was pure panic and very specifically connected to locking the door, and yet the act of not locking the door was part of a powerful ritual that represented the freedom that these trips offered.

These panic dreams propelled Blair out of bed and into the living room, where she would lock the front door as well as the sliding glass doors in the back. On the fourth night, she even took to sleeping on the couch, as she thought that if indeed there was something malevolent coming to the house, she wanted to be downstairs, where she would be in a better place to offer protection.

The dream on that night was even more upsetting, where the cabin they were in suddenly had a second-floor gallery where Blair could feel deliberate malevolence, a kind of "deliberate mischief," as she put it. Since Blair is such a powerful dreamer, she knows how to wake herself up in a disturbing dream, but as she attempted to do this in her dream state that night, the message from Spirit was very clear: "No, you cannot wake." She told me, "I would come up for half a second and then it was as if something energetically was giving me chloroform, like I was being strapped down for a surgery." On the fourth morning, she had had enough. The feeling that something evil was coming for Amanda was too great, and Blair told Amanda, "We've got to get you out of here."

At the time, nobody knew that Amanda was sick, not even Amanda. This trip was in May, and by June, she was diagnosed with stage-five glioblastoma, an inoperable tumor in the middle of her brain in the form of a star. The oncologists declared that they had never seen anything like it, and by the end of the month, Amanda had passed. Blair experienced tremendous phenomena as Amanda moved through the semicomatose twilight before she passed, as well as a sense of constant visitation since her passing. And though Blair's grief is epic, the connection that these two women shared in physical form is something that has not broken, like the "two sides of the same coin" of their shared dream. Amanda's passing is like that for Blair: one side is heartbroken at the loss, and the other feels the connection as eternal.

Not every friendship is blessed with such a vibrant and powerful connection as Blair shares with Amanda. The bonds of friendship and intimacy are powerful and operate in realms that are ultimately mysterious. These connections can be explored in dreamwork, using this concept of shared dreaming as an access to deepen your intuition and explore the mystical possibilities that dreams offer us to take waking-life connections and explore them in the dreamworld.

Chapter Four

Past Lives in Dreams

While listening to other people's dreams over the years, I have had a little whisper of a thought many times as I heard the details. The dreams I am speaking of have a certain fullness to them in terms of setting and circumstance, where there is an absence of the chaos found in typical dreaming. In a past-life dream, that setting would, of course, be in the past, and is often in a culture that is recognizable to the dreamer but different from the dreamer's waking-life world. The dream takes on a movie-like quality, and the dreamer feels like they are being presented with a slice of life, but in a very different setting and time frame. And the whispered thought I have is, "I think this dream may be reflecting a past life."

Most typical dreams are chaotic, with rapidly changing landscapes, irrational time frames, and the peculiar blending of wildly disparate images and sensations crashing into themselves in what we readily recognize as a dream. But sometimes dreams have a much more narrative sensibility, as if you were watching a movie. When a dream feels like it is telling a very complete story with characters and settings that feel like they might exist somewhere in another reality, you may be in a dream about a past life.

Do we have past lives? There are billions of people in the world who follow Hinduism or Buddhism, and both of these religions have reincarnation as a foundational tenet. There are Pagan religions that also favor this dynamic of death and rebirth as part of how consciousness exists. And though modern, New Age spiritually oriented organizations may not have reincarnation as a fundamental precept, it is quite fashionable to assume that past lives are a thing, and that we've all been other people in the past, where our consciousness is thought to have inhabited other bodies.

In the East, this is serious business, but no one is running around trying to find out if they were Cleopatra in a past life. The belief in reincarnation and karma is a sacred and powerful way of contextualizing the struggles of this life, but in a way that generates a perspective of continuity. The lessons you are learning now are a direct reflection of how well you learned them in your past life. One might consider that a past life, and the karma associated with it, may be directing how your current life is unfolding, but explorations of that do not take you into that past life; they ground you into the current life and the karmic lessons that come your way. The belief in karma and reincarnation inspires people in the present to do the best job they can to clear their karma in this life, but it does not typically result in a fascination with the past life. That is an invention of the West.

Where Am I? What Is This Place?

In my twenties I had a remarkably vivid dream that fits the description of a past-life dream, though it wasn't until ten years later that I had the validating experience that brought me back to the dream and what it might have meant. Let me start by saying that I knew I was not in a typical dream, and I had been paying attention to my dreams in an almost obsessive manner for about ten years at the time that I had it. Much of the dream was from a first-person point of view perspective, so I had the sense of seeing through the eyes of the witness of the dream. I had never been to London at that time in my life, but movies over the years gave me a visual clue to the location and time frame of where I was. It felt like England, and the manner of dress and horse-drawn carriages pegged it as sometime in the early nineteenth century.

The visual experience of this dream was wild. I would toggle back and forth between seeing the scene from an objective viewpoint interspersed with moments of first-person point of view perspective. And when I would slip inside the eyes of this individual, the visual image was of locking eyes with men I was passing on the street, and feeling a sexual urge rise up as I did. In real life, I was a young gay man at the height of the AIDS crisis. When I moved to New York City at twenty-one, sex was deadly, and I did not have the opportunity to explore my sexuality in any sort of organic way. Sex was confusing and scary to me, and this dream expressed a kind of sexual compulsivity that was not unlike what I had experienced as a young, vibrant gay man living in a world where exploring sex was frightening and the process was pretty shut down. This was the interpretation of the dream that satisfied me at the time.

Almost ten years after I had this dream, I found myself single and very interested in when my next relationship might come along. I sought out intuitive guidance, and during one reading, imagine my surprise when the reader let me know she was getting an image from a past life, and it seemed like she was watching the dream from all those years ago and describing what was happening. She mentioned London, described the era, the clothes, and my social status, and presented a life where I was a homosexual man in the early Victorian era, probably circa 1850. She went further than the little snapshot of my dream and recounted a life that ended badly because of being found out to be gay. The experience was powerful, and the way this reader was recounting the dream felt truthful because of how I felt in my body as I was sitting during this session.

This first-person point of view perspective was something that showed up in my research of other people's dreams of past lives. And while this is not to say that any such experience indicates a past-life dream, this perspective is unusual, and often memorable, and it may be a clue that such a dream is presenting itself.

Dena reached out and described such a dream that she had early one morning. She had already been awakened by her eight-year-old son, who had a habit of climbing into her bed for a morning snuggle with her. They had both fallen back asleep, and Dena had one of those twilight, in-between sort of dreams—not a middle-of-the-night REM story fest, but more a lucid, semiconscious dreaming experience.

I was transported in time to a dream that was first person, meaning I was the character, and I was seeing through the eyes of that character. It wasn't as if I was watching a scene play out like a movie; I was *in* the movie. I was walking along the side of a country road slowly and somberly. I felt exhausted but relieved, as if the weight of the world was lifted off me. I was with a group of people, and we were dressed in drab browns, very worn and torn clothing. I had a child by the hand. We were walking slowly, with our heads down, following those who were in front of us. There were people behind us as well. The road was to the right of us (we were on the shoulder of the road), and there was a thin row of trees separating the shoulder of the road from a large field.

It is this simultaneous awareness-of-the-scene perspective combined with a first-person point of view perspective that is one of the first signals that we may be in a past-life experience. Also, this was a sort of drop-in dream experience, one that did not rely on the slow churn through all the stages of sleep to get to REM, where images light up. This dream happened suddenly, while Dena was in this in-between state, not quite sleeping deeply but clearly not awake. The dream continued.

There were patches of snow on the ground, like it had been melting. As we slowly walked, I was looking down at my shoes. The earth beneath my feet was spongy; I could hear it squishing underfoot as we were sort of swaying back and forth as we walked. This is actually the memory of the dream that is the most vivid—the feeling of the earth under my feet, its softness and the sound of it. No one was talking. All you could hear were the steps of those walking on the earth. The field to my left had patches of snow as well, and there was the tiny hint of greenery coming through. Winter was melting away and spring was bursting through. The road to the right wasn't big. I can't be sure if it was even paved. It looked like a country road—no buildings, like a road that cut through farmland or rural areas. When I think about how it felt to hold that child's hand (I think a daughter), I felt incredibly relieved. And sad. We were walking away from something, and we were headed to an unknown, but it wasn't scary in any way.

Dena woke up and began to stir, coming back into consciousness and awakening to her son still cuddling next to her in bed. Seemingly out of the blue, her young child made a strange and out-of-context suggestion: "Mom, we should visit Israel." Dena asked why he would suggest this, and her son had no answer. In hindsight, Dena shared with me that she wondered if her child had been having some sort of shared dream experience that led him to make such a declaration. Having always had a strong pull toward Jewish culture, Dena is also a person who has a strong moral compass and a righteousness that causes a visceral reaction to anything relating to the Holocaust as well as anything exhibiting violence toward other humans.

Like so many of these mystical moments, we cannot know for certain what this dream experience was reflecting. The strong emotionality of the dream, the evocative imagery suggesting post-liberation events, and the almost non sequitur of her child's thoughts about a visit to Israel all led Dena to think that she had a vision of a past life during that lucid dream.

Past-Life Dreams Stay with Us

Brittany told me that during her childhood, she had horrific nightmares. Interestingly, although she did describe a rough home life, her nightmares featured graphic and violent images of war that most children wouldn't possibly have access to, including finding dead bodies, attempting to revive an injured person, and crying over a person with a missing limb. One key descriptor that Brittany offered seems to show up a lot with these types of dreams, which is that they have no discernible beginning or end. These scenes of war seemed like an ongoing narrative that Brittany was dropping into in the dream state, though her childhood self would not have had language for such observations. By the time she was eleven or twelve years old, Brittany had taken to researching both world wars of the twentieth century to somehow contextualize her nightmare images. The adults around her scoffed at such efforts, minimizing her nighttime experiences as just scary dreams, probably inspired by violent video games.

At fourteen years old, Brittany had a dream that would ultimately change the entire course of her life with regard to her inner experience. It is the most memorable dream that she has ever had, before or since, and it has never left her. There were several remarkable things about this dream as Brittany described it. For one thing, she was not awake, but also not asleep. Although her fourteen-year-old self might not have had any language for this experience, her adult self can describe this kind of dream lucidity. This quality was noteworthy enough to clue Brittany in to the notion that something unusual was taking place.

Another significant element of this powerful dream was how Brittany was relating to men in the dreams. In all of the war-torn landscapes of her previous dreams, the people in them were a random succession of humans, with Brittany feeling no direct connection to any of them. She would just visit this scenario in her nighttime experience, wake up in the morning, and move on.

Her dream started out as fairly typical. In it, she was right outside her childhood home, where she lived at the time. She had this urge in the dream where she knew that she had to stop someone from leaving, though she also had a sense that it might be too late. Then something interesting happened. She began to fly over her neighborhood to her junior high school in a manner that she described as simply allowing her head to follow her body and heart. When she arrived at this apparently significant destination, she saw a long line of strangers cued up and carrying luggage, almost as if they were lining up to get on a plane.

> I ran through the crowd to the front of the line, where I saw a man—wearing a military boot camp uniform, tan, with a chunky nose and a sharp jaw—and without any hesitation I forced him to turn around, and I hugged him. I hugged him so hard, and I don't remember speaking, but I felt that I would never see him again, like I was losing a lover, friend, someone I deeply, deeply loved. I telepathically told him I'd miss him and I loved him, and I felt him say it too. But for some reason I was okay with it, like I went through all the stages of grief with him in that moment of goodbye. As I started to cry and weep in his arms, I woke up—fourteen-year-old me—bawling my eyes out for this man, this

stranger. Out of all my dreams of war and horrific graphic events, this one stuck out—and hurt the most.

A little over a decade later, Brittany, who was now in her mid-twenties, had never stopped thinking about this dream. In fact, any time she met a man who was in the military, she would find herself wondering if she might match her dream soldier from all those years ago. And one day, she did. She met a young man who, after a few months of dating, showed Brittany pictures of himself when he was a bit younger, clean-shaven, and in boot camp. All Brittany could think about at that moment was that here was the man in her dreams from a decade ago. It turned out that this picture had been taken right before this young man almost died in a terrible car accident in which he was thrown out of his car, which was careening down the freeway at sixty miles per hour. He was pronounced dead on the scene by paramedics, but a little later he pulled out of his comatose state and survived to tell the tale.

Here's where it gets juicy: the timing of the accident matched the timing of the dream. This powerful synchronicity was actually a bit of an invitation. The rumbling intuitions around meeting this man and the uncanny connection to her dream led Brittany to explore all sorts of things like Reiki and energy work. She did some hypnosis to look into her energetic connection with this man and was eventually led to astrology. As an astrologer, I can tell you that there are very specific placements that can show up between two people's charts that indicate a past-life connection. The nodes of the Moon, the vectors of energy in the solar system that generate eclipses, show up in a birth chart as that person's karmic entry into this life as reflected by the South Node, and the person's life purpose and sense of destiny are indicated by the point opposite, the North Node. If two charts show any direct geometrical connections from points in one chart to the nodes in another chart, then those two people are thought to be connected through past-life consciousness. Brittany's and this man's charts reflected this type of deeper connection. There were even some interesting placements that showed up in this reading as indicators of some intensified action and violence orientation where notions of war fit the astrology through Mars, the planet named for the god of war.

The hypnosis session was even more revealing. Brittany describes having "an insane spiritually healing experience," in which she found herself talking with a past self who was, in fact, a man. In this previous life, this man had fought in World War II, and expressed tremendous guilt and shame for the things he had done, though he had no choice. He felt that he had let his wife and children down because he was unable to cope with the trauma that rose up after the war. In the Reiki session, the practitioner told Brittany that she was experiencing PTSD based on a past life, and of course she knew exactly which past life was the culprit, helping to explain the years of nightmares with war and battle as consistent, recurring images. Now, in the longer arc of Brittany's experience, the young man acted as more of a catalyst, and how he fits in in a multidimensional way is not quite clear. The impact of this experience on Brittany and how she lives her life now has been beyond transformational. Such is the power of mystical dreams.

Cassie, a woman now in her forties, had a dream when she was fifteen that has stuck with her ever since. In the dream, she was escaping from someone and ran into a barn to hide. She remembers the details very specifically: Stepping through the double doors. Bright sun clipping through the cracks of the door, disseminating shafts of light. Her, lying on the dirt of the barn floor wearing a long dress. She was definitely hiding from someone, either a boy or a man, with an unmistakable sense of terror that this person meant to hurt her. Cassie described the dream in this way:

> My mind went back and forth between being the one who was hiding from an abuser/killer/death and then somehow calmly watching all of it in third person. He never reached me before I woke up. When I came fully awake, I knew without a doubt that it had happened, but I didn't understand—still don't. I tried to go back to sleep to keep watching, but I lost it. There was so much fear that I felt and observed, and then somehow I was calm and unafraid as I reflected on it.

This dream felt so real to Cassie that she thought perhaps she was tapping into something in waking life that had happened in an actual barn near where she lived. Having grown up in a farming community, she certainly knew of many such barns on properties of friends of hers. This image was so powerful that she always kept an eye out in her travels, just in case she might someday actually see the barn from her dreams. Over time, the image lost some of its vibrancy in Cassie's memory, but even though her inner image has grown fuzzy over the years, the sensation of the memory in her body is as strong as it ever was. She wrote to me that she feels quite convinced of the power of this memory. She said, "Without a doubt, what I saw was a moment in time that occurred. I was there, somehow. I was watching and being watched by myself at the same time. The experience has simply stuck with me. I believe in the unseen and unknown, and that dream only strengthens my fascination with all the things I can't quite figure out."

April is a woman who is no stranger to the power of dreams. Like so many of the people who shared their experiences with me, she has lived her life in the pursuit of higher consciousness and self-actualization. She has had a recurring dream throughout her life that appears to be revealing a specific scenario that, much like many people have reported to me, seems as if it has a constancy to it. Although these dream experiences have been sporadic, each time she visits this landscape, she has a powerful sense that she is visiting the same place.

When April first started having these dreams, in some of them, she felt herself to be a boy, and in others, a girl, but these dream images always reflected youthful embodiment. There was a decidedly Native American feel to the scenario, and April is fairly certain that this village she periodically visited in her dreams was one that actually existed in an earlier time and place. But always, and with complete consistency, she perceived herself to be a young boy or girl in these dreams.

This changed dramatically in 2011, and may have connected to a relationship that rose up in April's adult life. There was a man who came into April's life through her work community, and the circumstances were such that every spring he would

come into her orbit for an annual event that needed his attention. The first year they met, there was an instant sense of the
two of them clicking. But it was during the second year that
the connection solidified as they both shared that they'd had a
strong sense of anticipation about seeing each other again. The
two lived in separate areas of the United States, and the connection was ultimately not a romantic one, but their friendship
extended outside of the work-related connection that brought
them together in the first place. April described the dream scenario like this.

> I am in a Native American village along a river. The only
> threats are natural and warring tribes. I am a female in my
> twenties and fairly pregnant. It is coming into fall, and my
> daily routines are rising in the morning, combing and plait-
> ing my partner's hair, going downstream to cleanse myself,
> preparing a morning meal for myself and my husband,
> then joining a large group of women working hides, mak-
> ing clothes, and laughing. Often my partner sneaks over
> to see me, and often I sneak away to spend time with him.
> There are horseback rides and walks, groups by the fire. We
> are young and happy in a way I have no words to describe.

April's memory of this dream fits all the things that turn out
to be typical in past-life dreams. First, the adult scenario of this
dream is directly connected to the many years of tapping into
this landscape where she typically felt much younger. It was
definitely the same village she had visited many times before,
only it evolved, and she was now an adult, experiencing adult-
like things. She continued:

Suddenly it is dark, and my partner is gone to a war party. I am not in my lodge, but in the woman's lodge, in labor. I remember crying out over and over to see my partner one last time. Then I am a hawk circling in the sky above, and it is winter. A man sits before what I know is my lodge. He is alone and without clothes. He refuses anyone who attempts to help him. I land and try to tell him I am there, but he pushes me away. I fly high into the sky, and he is there flying next to me.

Now the dream seems to meld into something that is simultaneously literal and symbolic. The way this dream ends appears to have a message that goes beyond this one life in the village. It offers imagery that suggests a connection between souls that transcends that one life. When, the next morning after this dream, April received an out-of-the-blue text from her work friend, it was natural to share with him this very intense dream she had just had. After comparing notes, it turned out that they had had what was pretty much the same dream, in another example of mystical dreams of different structure overlapping as a way we humans connect to the mystery. These two humans have never stopped being in touch, and they both believe with utter conviction that they were in fact the same couple that they dreamed of. And I believe them too.

You will recognize Eli from the description of his lucid dreams in chapter 2 of this book, as his mystical relationship with his dreamworld started when he was only three years old. Of course, his three-year-old self didn't know anything about past lives. He had consistent experiences of waking up and having a sensation that he was different people. He understood this in a very childlike manner at the time, but the adult Eli can put language to those very early experiences. He can describe a sense of knowing that was present at age three, but with time and perspective, he can well and clearly describe the experience at seventy-three. In fact, he now has a word for the mysterious place in his dreams in those early childhood nighttime experiences where he would connect with myriads of humans. He calls it the "pool of souls." And in his little boy consciousness, he began to recognize individuals who would show up.

So little Eli, living with his brother and their parents in a tiny apartment in Brooklyn where he slept on a small bed behind the living room bookshelf, would wake up having dreams of these different humans in this pool of souls. In these bizarre dream landscapes, he felt that he *was* these people, as the experience of dreaming of them was really an internal experience of witnessing the dream through them. In one dream, he found himself living in a jungle setting.

> I had one other recurring dream starting at the same age. I walk into a room, huge room. I'm a man, maybe in my fifties. From the opposite end of the room, a woman walks in who I know is my daughter. And then someone stabs me in the back and I die. I started having that dream when I was three, over and over and over again. And when I was in fourth grade, I opened my new social studies book on the first day—they give you a whole sack of your new books— and in the upper left-hand corner of the left page was a drawing of a reconstruction of a house in ancient Egypt, and it wasn't the exact same house [from my dreams], but

it was like, "Oh my god, that's the house." I never saw anything like that house ever in my life.

In yet another dream, Eli was part of a family living in a
huge mansion filled with servants. He woke up from the dream
with this odd sensibility of being two people at once, himself
and the person he had dreamed of, which led him to ask his
mother what had happened to his other parents. This question
seemed to enrage Eli's mother, so he never spoke again about
these dream experiences.

Eli, with his very young perspective of life in a tiny home in
an urban location, could not have known anything about man-
sions and jungles, so the first-person sensibility of these dreams
was remarkable, and he would rouse from his dreams feeling
as if he actually were these individuals from the dreams. One
morning—and of course this has stayed with Eli his entire life—
he "woke up" thinking to his witness self, "Oh, you're the little boy who lives in the three-room apartment with your little
brother and ..." Although he initially identified this individual
from the pool of souls as "other" within the dream, he eventually realized that he was that soul, and this was the life he was
currently living.

It was not until Eli was in his twenties that he stumbled upon
a book that offered the context he needed to understand his
early childhood dreams. The rather literal title of the book was
Children's Past Lives, where the author interviewed people from
cultures that readily accept the idea of reincarnation. Had this
been the case for young Eli, the reportage of these experiences
would likely have led to his mother sitting down and drawing

out the content of these dreams instead of the passive-aggressive anger that she expressed.

Finally, let's look at the experiences of Annie, whose lifetime of appreciating and honoring her dreams has been a driving force in her self-exploration. Like so many people who have had childhood dreams that may actually be past-life expressions, Annie saw images in dreams she had when she was only five or six years old that would later, in her adult life, hit her like a shot when those same images came into her view in the waking world.

In this recurring dream, Annie would find herself on a wooden bunk, looking out into the space she was occupying, which was a room filled with wooden bunks such that the one she was on was flanked by many others in this space. She could perceive herself in the dream as healthy, ruddy-cheeked, and about the same age as she was in real life at the time she was having the dream. The sensation she had was not at all nefarious, but more curiosity as to where she was, why she was there, and where the others who ought to be occupying the other bunks were. This dream, which recurred quite a bit in those years, did not land as a nightmare, but the images from the dreams were powerful enough to stay with her for her entire life.

Both Annie's mother and her grandmother had direct experience of the Holocaust, and were, in fact, survivors of the concentration camp at Buchenwald. As such, knowledge about this moment in history would eventually be very much a part of Annie's awareness. But by the time Annie turned five, there had been no open discussions about the family history. Her mother chose to never discuss it with her, and certainly the realities of the Holocaust and life in a concentration camp were completely unavailable to Annie at this young age. The Americans liberated the camps in 1945, and Annie was born seven years after that. Many years later, Annie stumbled upon pictures of these camps that were taken by the soldiers who liberated them. The haunting vision of rows and rows of wooden bunks, where three to four emaciated prisoners were crammed into slots built for one human, was instantly recognizable to Annie as the image from her recurring dream.

Chapter Five

Visitation Dreams

The greatest mystery of existence itself is death. Without death, life could not exist, but the very notion of the awareness that death will end our lives is the source of the existential crisis that all humans must face. As a psychologist, I was taught in grad school that the fear of death is what underlies all conflict in our waking lives, as deep below the surface of our unconscious minds, this fear is absolute. As a scientist, I accept this as a true statement about the human condition. But I am not just a scientist. I am also half mystic, and if I put that hat on, I have a very different idea of the terror that death presents us with, and what happens deep below the surface of our conscious awareness.

Everything in our perception of existence can be expressed as a binary. There is up and down, in and out, right and left, day and night. And, of course, the fundamental binary is life and death. We are unconscious beings who have a conscious mind that helps us navigate our experience in the world, further illuminating this binary as also including conscious and unconscious. All these pairings can also be considered as either masculine or feminine in nature. There is a tradition in the world of symbolism that left is feminine and right is masculine. Daytime, replete with sunlight, is the masculine expression of the day, whereas the feminine domain is the dark of night, which has an astrological corollary to the Sun representing the masculine presence and the Moon being the luminary of night.

If we push this notion into the question of life and death, we can understand life as the masculine aspect of existence and death as the feminine aspect. This makes sense, too, when we consider that death and birth are essentially the same thing, and in this model, life as masculine is on one side of the binary, and on the other side is not just death, but death and rebirth. If we add to this recipe the element of sleeping and dreaming, then wakefulness is masculine and the sleeping and dreaming state is feminine. So sleeping and death, and waking and life, are related. In fact, it could be said that every night when we go to sleep, we are experiencing a metaphorical death, and we are reborn each time we wake up from a deep sleep.

These three things share the same sensibility: sleep, dreams, and death. Our thinking mind is the narrator and navigator of our waking life. As we drop into the sleep state, that part of our brain is shut off, like a mini death of our conscious awareness, which is restored each morning as our brain activity fires up once again. We can put the thinking mind in the opposite category, so the realm of sleep, dreams, and death is more akin to the absence of the thinking mind. Perhaps for the sake of this discussion, we can call this the dreaming mind. The dreaming mind is not subject to the limitations of the wakeful, thinking mind, and since sleep and dreams are the realm of the unconscious and therefore death, we come to the conclusion that the closest we can get to death while still alive and in a body is to go to sleep and dream.

If you follow this thread of logic, there can be little resistance to the notion that if there is any possibility of crossing through the thin veil between life and death, it would happen in dreams more than anywhere else. The term *medium* refers to someone who has a kind of direct access to whatever dimension people who have made their transition from life into death are in. There are many people who have such a clear, intuitive connection to such realms that when they are holding space with a person, they can easily connect to that person's loved ones who have died. The ability to open up to these other dimensions is also a kind of wiring in the psyche, and there are those who can access these realms with greater ease than others.

Dreams Open the Veil Between Life and Death

One such person who shared their experiences with me is Teresa, who said she has had many dreams with people who have passed away. One phrase she used was interesting to me because it somewhat validates the notion I have put forth, that visitation dreams have a certain structure to them not shared by typical, chaotic narrative dreaming. She described these experiences as "people who have passed away walking right on through" her dreams.

Teresa has a strong spiritual practice and has worked in her adult life as a tarot card reader and a Reiki master, so her day-to-day life offers the opportunity to continuously flex her intuitive muscles. As is the case for many who do this sort of work for others, Teresa's early childhood was tumultuous and traumatizing, but at seven years old a powerful vision of what she described as a visiting angel helped her get in touch with an inner, mystical power, and this vision changed everything for her. There was even a tea leaf–reading grandmother who recognized Teresa's gifts and gave her the language to describe it as her "knowing," though it would be years before she truly understood what that meant. By the time Teresa was in her twenties, she owned her first deck of tarot cards and began making a direct correlation between her waking life and intuitive experiences that came to her in her dream life, which often connected her to people who had recently passed away.

While this intuitive connection occurs with people in her personal life, it is more likely to happen to Teresa the night following a tarot card reading or Reiki session involving a client. In fact, she typically opens up her energy field to the energy field of the client to start the session, but often will deliberately not close it up for a specific reason. Sometimes, as in the example below, by keeping those channels open, the reading will continue into the nighttime experience of Teresa's dreams.

During the first few months of the COVID-19 lockdown, a young woman went to Teresa for a tarot reading. Through her medium sensitivity, Teresa felt that some sort of energetic entity accompanied the client, and Teresa immediately felt that this was the client's father. While this client appeared to Teresa to be too young to have lost her father, she confirmed that her father had in fact passed away a few months prior to the session, and that due to COVID-19 restrictions, it aggrieved her that she had not been able to be with him and see him before he passed.

That evening while sleeping, Teresa was having a dream that was like any other. In the middle of whatever narrative was playing out, the same man from the session, her client's father, appeared in her dream. As the dream continued, he had a message for his daughter. Interestingly, the father approached Teresa with his hands crossed over his mouth, but nonetheless, she could her him in her mind. He said the following:

> I didn't get to say goodbye. I have so many words to share. Please tell my girl that I will always be with her. Tell her to go to our favorite beach when the winds are strong. Tell her to sit in our spot, looking out to sea. I will come to her, and the winds will carry my words to her.

Teresa often feels quite full in her heart when such dreams happen, which was certainly the case here. She called her client the next morning and found that she, the client, was deeply moved just by the story. After a time, the client reported that she did indeed go to that beach on a windy day and had a profound feeling of connection to her father, and the howling winds did in fact deliver a beautiful heartfelt message.

One does not have to be a professional medium to have powerful visitation dream experiences. In fact, the abundance of anecdotal evidence of such phenomena reinforces the likelihood that these experiences are a fundamental aspect of the human consciousness. When I reached out to my community asking for them to share with me their various mystical dream experiences for this book, this topic was the one that got the most responses. There were so many amazing stories people shared with me.

Patricia lost her father in the mid-1990s and was aggrieved during his passing because his condition rendered him unavailable for affection and she was aching to hug him one last time. A few days after his passing, he showed up in her dream state, where he gave her that hug she wanted so badly.

Alys shared a dream of being in a grassy field filled with daisies, where her beloved dog, Red, came running toward her, just after she'd had to put him down in waking life. The difficult passage she was moving through at that time was made more comfortable by her ongoing sensation of Red's presence around her, and it was this dream that established that sense of connection.

When Siblia's father died when she was just nineteen, she was unable to afford an airline ticket to get her back for the funeral. A very clear dream that she described as more of an "inner experience" allowed her to connect with and say goodbye to her father in a way that was just as powerful as, if not more powerful than, if she had been able to attend the funeral in person.

It seems clear that this phenomenon is fairly ubiquitous, and I believe this is an experience that may be common to most, if not all, human beings. After all, so much of our dreaming experience is relegated to the unconscious, and we lose the tether to the richness of our dreams in the abyss of the deep recesses of the mind, far below the level of wakeful awareness. Such dreams can have a tremendous influence on the dreamer, especially as it relates to the specific process of grieving the lost loved one. In fact, the sense of being visited in a dream can be so powerful that it can have a revolutionary and transformative impact on their personal belief systems.

One such dreamer is a young man I had a conversation with many years ago who was struggling tremendously after the death of his grandmother. She had been his primary caretaker, and her death was the first big loss in his life. He shared a story with me of a moment that was completely transformative for him. What happened to him after she died affected him on a level he barely understood, but generated a paradigm shift for him of epic proportions.

Immediately after his grandmother's death, Jonathan drove from Los Angeles to San Diego to be with his family for the funeral. While he was driving, he felt dangerously sleepy, and for his own safety, he exited the freeway, got a little snack, and found a secluded place to park his car and take a nap. He immediately fell into a deep sleep and found himself in a dream landscape. The dream was that he was sleeping in his car, but then he woke up to find that he was parked under a large tree, and his grandmother was standing underneath this tree. Suddenly the car was gone, and he was just standing with his grandmother in the shade of this enormous tree, and while nothing was said, the felt sensation of the dream was blissful and filled him with a peace that he had not felt since learning of her death.

Jonathan told me this story with tears in his eyes, but it wasn't the dream content that stuck with me. After all, by this time, I had heard many dozens of such stories. It was the change in him, the transformational shift that just having this dream opened him up to, that struck me. Before this moment, he had never had an experience of connecting to other dimensions in a past life. This was a paradigm shift for him, and I knew that at that moment, he had crossed a threshold into an awareness of the mystery of life that would leave him forever changed. It put him on a path that might lead to more spiritual expansion in the remaining years of his life, because his mind and heart were opened up in this initial transformation experience of his grandmother's passing.

Grandmothers seem to be a prominent figure in a lot of visitation dreams. I believe that because the matriarchal role of care is such a key factor in how most people feel loved and nurtured, grandmothers can often be a source of great love and sustenance. In fact, because the pressure of parenting is lifted on that older generation, it can often be the case where grandmothers offer a more direct sense of love and care, and their advanced age necessitates an early experience of loss for many people. As such, it was not surprising that many of the stories shared with me about visitation dreams involved grandmothers. This was certainly true for Lori, who shared a visitation dream with me that involved her grandmother.

Like many people who have this experience, Lori was very close to her grandmother when she was a girl. She spent every summer with her grandmother in the village where she grew up. The bond was very strong between them in life, but because Lori has a strong spiritual underpinning to how she lives her life, that bond remained powerful even after her grandmother's passing. In what was perhaps a case of glorious synchronicity, just as I was asking people in my circles to share such dreams with me, Lori had this dream just a few days before receiving my email asking for dream stories. Here is what she described:

In my dream, I found myself in a room with dim light. The room had no furniture or ornaments whatsoever. The only objects in the room were a few chairs placed in a circular way, simple chairs (like we used to have at my birth home). Right away, I found myself in the middle of this circle, surrounded by the chairs, and at that moment I realized that all of my grandma's sisters (who had passed away) and some other women were sitting on these chairs.

I love this image of all the woman gathered together, as it seems to reflect the continuity that bridges the connection between us and our ancestors. Just as so many stories of people moving toward the light in near-death experiences usually include family members who have already made their transition, with visitation dreams we come to understand that while it may defy our sense of logic and form, our ancestors are likely hanging out with each other beyond the veil. In Lori's dream, they were clearly planning some sort of meeting.

I felt my grandmother's presence next to me. (She was the alpha in my family.) Next to her appeared her aunt. (She truly was the super alpha, and my grandma and all of her sisters always looked up to her. She was a fearless, independent woman.) At that moment, my dear grandmother asked her aunt if she could teach me how to waltz. The aunt agreed silently, gently placing one hand on my back, the other holding my hand, and we started to dance together. She was leading the dance, showing me all the moves. Then I woke up.

Lori woke from this dream and explained that she felt as if she had just come out of a powerful ritual where some sort of life passage was being honored. It was an interesting thing to note that in the dream, it was not her direct ancestor, her grandmother, who was offering the instructions on how to dance her life into joy. Grandma was there to provide the loving protection needed for Lori to receive the blessing bestowed on her by the true matriarch of the clan, her great-aunt. The last thing that Lori expressed to me was perhaps the most powerful: "I felt that powerful ancestor connection, and realized right then and there that I am never alone. The blood of my ancestors was awakened in me. The blood of these strong women runs in me. Truly grateful to this dream."

When Stacy was eleven years old, her grandmother died. While it is not uncommon for grandparents to transition early in someone's life, Stacy describes her grandma as meaning the world to her. Growing up in a household that was very dysfunctional, Stacy explained that her divorced parents were rarely able to provide the emotional stability that any child might need, and for the first years of Stacy's life, her grandmother was the only source of care that left her feeling loved and that her needs were being met. Stacy said to me, "So when she died, I thought my world was ending. I was in so much pain, I would stand in her closet and hug her clothes just so I could feel like I was hugging her. I remember thinking to myself that there was *no way* I was going to make it through life without her."

Several months after her passing, Stacy's grandmother visited Stacy in her dreams. She describes it as the most vivid technicolor dream she has ever had, before or since. The setting was a beautiful garden, which in retrospect made sense to Stacy because her grandmother loved gardening so much, and in fact the garden was a location where Stacy and her grandma had connected when she was alive. I will add here that the garden is known to be a common setting in visitation dreams. In Stacy's dream, she and her grandmother were sitting together on a bench in this gorgeous, colorful landscape that seemed to include every color of flower imaginable.

The content of the dream was right in alignment with just about all visitation dreams, where a message is delivered. "She told me that she was okay. She also told me that I was going to be fine in the world and that she would watch over me and help me from the other side," Stacy reported. This message was very simple, and in fact the simplicity of the message is a hallmark of all visitation dreams. The impact of this message on Stacy was transformative, as she still remembers waking up from the dream and feeling what she described as "immeasurable peace." The dream changed her and gave her the confidence to go on with her life, and the feeling that she was dying a little every day lifted. It has been forty years since that dream, and Stacy can still tap into the memory of it as powerfully today as when it first arrived.

As I mentioned with Stacy's dream, the garden as a setting is quite common in visitation dreams. But there was something in her dream that is even more ubiquitous, and that is the presence of a bench of some sort. As a symbol that might appear in any dream, a bench has a meaning that connects to things that occur incongruously and out of time. In an urban setting, the presence of a bench invites a person to sit, taking them out of the organic flow of whatever they are doing or wherever they are heading. If the bench is located in a park or a garden, then the bench takes on the meaning of the capacity to take in something of beauty and contemplate it in a way that needs no goal or purpose connected to it. In this way, I think benches appear in a lot of visitation dreams because we all have this unconscious association with benches as a place where the flow of life stops and something that can only be available with stillness and rest can be experienced.

The Proverbial Bench in Visitation Dreams

Brian wrote to me about a dream he had with his father who passed away after being hospitalized for many months when Brian was fifteen years old. A short time after the funeral, Brian had a dream that took place on a beautiful blue-sky sort of day. There was nothing in this setting but green grass as far as Brian could see. There was a sense that Brian was moving in this dream, and as he traversed a slight upgrade in the landscape, there appeared in the near distance a bench, the proverbial dream bench that I have been speaking of. Brian and his father sat on the bench and talked for a few minutes, after which his father said it was time for him to leave. At this point, his father began to levitate, to rise up and hover at just about shoulder height to Brian in a manner that looked like he was holding his body in a Superman flying posture, while at the same time he was drifting and slowly ascending to a higher level. Brian wanted him to stay, but his father kept repeating that it was his time to go. And while that scenario might not seem like it would be a satisfying conclusion to the visit, Brian woke up and had a sense of contentment that not only was a great help in his grief, but also planted a seed of consciousness that would set teenage Brian up for an adulthood filled with spiritual exploration.

Another bench motif visitation dream came from Ann, whose grandmother came to visit in a dream that took place in a nebulous setting, but the bench in the dream reminded her of the kind you might see in a cemetery. Their relationship in life was important to Ann, as Grandma was intuitive and a little mystical, and one of the focuses of her gifts was connected to handwriting. Besides having general intuitive moments, such as predicting the death of a loved one after being visited by what she referred to as "the shadow of death" when someone close was making their transition, Grandma could also get accurate impressions of people's energy through their handwriting. In fact, Ann and her grandmother used to look through letters together that she would receive, trying to either recognize the handwriting by itself or dropping into the energy of the hand-writing in order to get an intuitive sense of the author. Toward the end of Grandma's life, while she was living in a nursing home due to a stroke, Ann even helped her practice her writing, so she had a very good sense of recognition when it came to her grandmother's script.

So we have this dream that features some of the key factors that support the notion that it was a visitation. It had a single setting, a kind of cemetery-like environment, and also a bench, which is often a symbol of important moments out of the normal flow of life's movement. This was no ordinary visual visitation dream, as Grandma did not appear as an etheric avatar. Instead, in the dream, Ann read a letter, which she absolutely knew to be from her grandmother, as the handwriting was a perfect match. The message was also standard for a visitation dream, as Ann herself indicated: "I knew it was her because she wrote me a note and said, 'All is well and I'm fine here.'"

Now let's explore what can happen when a visitation dream features the untimely death of someone younger, rather than an elder. One of the more moving examples of a visitation dream came from Leslee, a woman who lost her seventeen-year-old son to suicide. This story is compelling not only because of the depth of the pain contained within it, but also because the dream experience itself has some interesting complexity, as it was also a "dream within a dream" experience. Leslee had this dream exactly eighty-one days after her son's passing, and she describes the dream as bringing her a tremendous amount of comfort that she feels to this day, years later.

The first part of Leslee's dream was pure visitation, following all the structural rules outlined at the top of this chapter. It had a single scenario, and it included one of the leading indicators that a visitation is playing out, which is when the dream itself seems to be taking place in the room that the dreamer is sleeping in. Leslee described it like this:

> Sometime in the early morning I woke up to see Joshua at the foot of the bed. He was dressed in his Levi's, gray Central Catholic T-shirt, and wearing his glasses. I got up and hugged him and said, "Josh, is that really you?" He said, "Of course it is, Mom!" He took my hand and then I fell back into a deep sleep.

This felt so much like waking life, Leslee even used the phrase "I woke up" to set the scene. Clearly, her deceased son sitting on her bed is all the evidence we need to know that it was a dream and that she had not actually woken up. This level of her dreaming consciousness was enough to connect her to her son. Once they made contact, her psyche brought her to an experience that I would call a more standard dream, where Leslee was connecting to her own deep psyche, and that was more about the personal experience of connecting with her son at a deeper level of her psyche. Here is the dream within a dream that came next, in her own words.

> I dreamed I was in his room, but it wasn't his room here in this house. I found a small bag of chocolates left over from Christmas. There was kind of a nook in the room and I sat down to eat the candy and was looking at all the toys in his room, a toy parking garage, trucks, and cars. I felt so very sad looking at it all. Then he appeared out of nowhere. He was about nine years old and he was wearing an all-white space suit. I could see his sweet face through his visor. He took my hand in his gloved hand and I believe we traveled through space together. I'm not sure because I don't remember that part. We came back to the nook in his room though, and he said he had to leave. I asked if I could kiss him goodbye and he lifted the visor so I could kiss his cheek. I still feel his soft cheek on my lips. I was so filled with joy when I saw him and held his hand. As he left, he winked at me and said telepathically, "You don't mind cleaning up my room, do you?" I remember sobbing in the dream after he left.

This dream is pure personal psyche working things out. Now Leslee is in his room, which can be interpreted as the compartment within her own psyche that contains the consciousness of her son and their relationship. Christmas is so vibrantly connected with childhood, and the joy of Christmas can be profound for children whose families celebrate this holiday. Even the candy and toy trucks are powerful images that reflect the joys of childhood. The space suit is interesting because it combines both a childhood symbol of self-expression through costumes and the notion that since Joshua is no longer in a body, he is in fact more an astronaut than a pedestrian, if you allow the image of space to represent his deeper connection to the realm of spirit. If you recall, Leslee told us her dream took place exactly eighty-one days after his death. If you add the digits together, eight plus one, you get nine, the number of completions and endings in numerology. Even the parting shot of the request to clean his room is a symbol reflecting the ways in which mothers serve their children's needs as part of the relationship agreement.

The power of this nighttime experience continued into Leslee's waking life when the next morning, she noticed that the very first image on her social media feed was an image of astronauts, and this synchronicity was not lost on her. Leslee is also someone who regularly practices various techniques of what we call active imagination, where we use more creative processes to work with dream imagery in an irrational way. In fact, seeing the image on her feed was active imagination in process. Active imagination is a way of consciously working with the unconscious mind, a technique developed by Carl Jung, the father of modern dreamwork. During the early twentieth century, this Swiss psychologist developed meditative techniques through which the material in a person's unconscious can be translated into images, narratives, personified as internal archetypal characters that make up the personality as a whole. This can serve as a bridge between the conscious ego and the unconscious.

"Imagination Is More Important Than Knowledge."—Albert Einstein

In a general way, active imagination can include any process by which the rational mind is quieted down and creativity is allowed to guide the process of self-investigation. The original intervention that Jung created, which he called active imagination, starts with a writing process where one sits down with pen and paper and formulates a question that is directed toward the unconscious mind. To receive the answer, one must switch hands and put the pen in the non-dominant hand, and that act alone triggers a different part of the psyche when pen is put to paper. This is a great technique to use in dreamwork, especially when a character appears in a dream that feels important but perhaps still mysterious, as dreams can be. In such a case, I might instruct the dreamer to sit down and do a dialogue with that character in this fashion: question posed with the dominant hand, then switch hands for the answer. The results can be quite surprising and illuminating.

Leslee took this to a deeper level by sitting down to have a conversation with the inner Joshua by writing questions on a piece of paper with her dominant hand, then switching to her non-dominant hand for the answers. She wrote, "Where did we go on the trip we took last night?" After switching hands, she replied with, "To the rainbow stars," an answer that contains an interesting reference to the Rainbow Bridge, a symbol often used to describe the process of a soul crossing over into spirit form after death. She also did one of the most powerful things we can ever do with a dream image, which is to be creatively expressive with the symbolism from a dream. By doing something creative, not only was she able to make deeper personal distinctions about her process of grief, but the drawing was able to bring her enormous comfort as she learned how to integrate this new level of grief.

Jacquelyn had been estranged from her parents for a number of years when her father died, a separation that had actually been initiated by her parents, based on their objection to challenges that Jacquelyn was having in her marriage. She was an only child, and the enforced separation was devastating to her at the time. Several months after the situation reached a crisis, Jacquelyn attempted to reconnect with her father, and even suggested that they needed to fix this divide before one of them died. Her father was unmoved, stating that there could be no reconciliation between them unless and until Jacquelyn addressed issues in her own marriage, fueling tremendous rage in our dreamer.

Four years after the estrangement was initiated, a knock on the door from Jacquelyn's aunt delivered the information that her father had indeed died before the two of them could attempt a reconciliation. This translated to a rageful response to the loss, a not-uncommon reaction when a parent dies before forgiveness has been found. Jacquelyn was knocked over by this news, and a few hours after it had been unceremoniously delivered, she took a nap. She was jolted awake after seeing an image of her father that she described like this:

> [It was] not really a dream, just this blast of a huge image. Envisioning a movie screen, it covered the whole screen. Similar to an image that would be in a portrait. His expression was the same as in a portrait we had made when I was in sixth grade, and he was wearing the same brown suit jacket. The image that jolted me awake was just the top of his shoulders and his head. He was looking forward, as though he was looking at me, and a bright, bright yellow glow was behind him, with the lighter glow all around him, similar to that which is depicted in many spiritual pictures as an aura or essence.

There was great comfort in this dream image, and Jacquelyn found her face streaming with tears as she lay on her couch, desperately attempting to hold onto the powerful image, only to have it disappear in that way that dreams are so utterly ephemeral. And while this experience did indeed offer some inner comfort to Jacquelyn, the funeral itself was triggering to her, and further emphasized the rift between our dreamer and her biological family.

What came to Jacquelyn in the dream state was a visitation that inserted itself into a standard dream experience. In the dream, she found herself in a kind of observer mode, and walking through corridors that both reminded her of high school and also included a sense of spiritual reverence, as if this location were sacred ground as well. Some of the corridors were dilapidated and showing signs of past wear and tear, while others were clean and pristine. She found herself moving through many of the corridors, searching intently for her father, who she could feel was nearby.

This felt like a psyche dream where hallways represent transitions in life, and certainly stepping into grieving a parent is a new and rather significant hallway-of-life experience. The old hallways were past moments of change, and perhaps the new, untried corridors represented the current ways that life was putting Jacquelyn into a process of great change. At the end of the dream, there was another scenario that felt to me like our dreamer working out personal conflicts, but this middle section was pure visitation.

We know that this is a visitation dream because of the single setting principle. When Jacquelyn finally saw her father in the dream in the distance, she ran to him and they embraced. The dream took on this quality of connection, physical embrace, and the peace and comfort that filled her increased as she could feel them both leaning into the hug. She felt held, and while she couldn't actually hear any words in this exchange, the felt sense was that they were communicating powerfully. There was a sense of ease and joy in this moment, and the sense of animation and exuberance was actually not something that her father had been available for during his life. The way she described this part of the dream was like every single visitation experience that so many dreamers have shared. And in the blink of a dreamlike eye, the bubble was burst and he was gone.

Then we return to the pedestrian elements of the dream, where the frantic sensations of typical dreams return, and Jacquelyn finds herself once again running through the symbolic corridors of her psyche. The dream turns from visitation back to the dream reflecting her psyche and the tremendous stress that the loss of her father was putting her through. Now the dream was more reflective of waking-life conflicts, for she was frantically searching and calling for her father, but when she connected to him in this section of the dream, he was no longer acknowledging her presence. When she tracked his gaze, she could see what he was fixated on, which was her mother, kneeling at a table in a posture that reminded Jacqueline of devotion at an altar.

The implication is clear: Jacquelyn's father was urging her to move toward her mother in forgiveness. We are no longer in visitation mode, and this interaction feels to me to be more about Jacquelyn's inner father archetype and not the spirit of her actual father beyond the veil. The rage returned, and the dream now reflected a frantic search for her father, only for her to be led back to the place where her mother was kneeling in supplication. And though the angry feelings remained, our dreamer finished the dream kneeling silently beside her mother, closing her eyes and adopting a prayerful position, eyes closed and head bowed. Reconciliation was reflected in the body posture, with seething rage in her heart. Truly, this is the beginning of the possibility for true forgiveness.

Let's explore an example of a visitation dream that involves a married couple. Susan and Bruce were married for twenty-two years. Bruce had an interesting journey that included some difficult health challenges that ultimately led to his death. At the center of these difficulties was a case of severe scoliosis due to a botched childhood surgery. Bruce lived a vibrant life that even included some significant physical labor, as he spent much of his adult life in the theater, behind the scenes in many different capacities. In the middle of his journey, he spent some years as a substance abuse counselor, but returned to spend his last years working once again in the realm that he loved so much, as a stagehand in the theater.

Bruce's life was limited by his physicality, yet he managed to spend much of his journey in a significantly physical way, as life behind the scenes in the world of theater is extremely demanding on the body. During his theatrical career, he did many different jobs, from box pusher to electrician, set builder, and lighting technician and designer. Through the course of his vibrant career in stagecraft, what he loved the most was lighting dancers. In fact, he confessed that in his heart of hearts, if he could have done one thing that was, ultimately, elusive for him due to the limitations of his body, he would have been a dancer himself.

When Susan and Bruce met, he was in his addiction counselor phase, but at a certain point he returned to his first love to work as a stagehand. As Bruce aged, his scoliosis worsened, and he had to retire from show business. The challenges of his body impacted his digestion and his ability to breath, and he passed away at the age of fifty-six. Susan was devastated, as this had been a long marriage, and she described their relationship as being one where they were each other's favorite person, and occasionally they even heard each other's thoughts. The connection ran deep and the loss was profound, and Susan immediately felt adrift. Her favorite person was gone, and even the cessation of her role as caregiver left her feeling quite alone, so much so that she described losing her faith, something that had always been a foundational element of her life.

Part of why this loss of faith rose up after Bruce's passing was that a few years prior, Susan had had what she described as an unexpected mystical experience while holding their first cat as she crossed over the Rainbow Bridge. This had been such a vibrant experience, and when Bruce passed, Susan longed for, and perhaps even expected, something similar to occur. When it did not, she was left feeling adrift, totally alone, and in deep grief.

> Then one night a couple of months later, I had a brief but vivid dream. I saw Bruce standing straight and tall in a full-body leotard on a stage next to a lake. It was that moment just before a dancer begins to move, and his face was peaceful and serene. That was all there was to the dream, but I knew it was a message that he was okay.

What I particularly love about this story is that the dream follows all the rules of visitation dreams, with a single setting and a nonverbal message that all is well. The added dimension of Bruce appearing to Susan in a physical state that transcended his lived experience of a body that had hindered his freedom reflects the beauty of what happens when we transcend our body and live in Spirit. This dream had a very big impact on Susan, especially as it related to her personal relationship with her own spirituality, something that had always been a vibrant part of her journey. The loss of Bruce put her into a state of crisis where that element of her humanity felt lost to her, but only temporarily, of course, as this dream experience woke her up once again to the deeper experience of this life. She reports that since then, she has become even more open to her intuition and the messages of guidance that she receives as she moves through her life.

Not every visitation dream involves blood relations, and plenty of the stories I collected were from people who experienced powerful and transformative visitations involving beloved individuals who were not genetic relatives. Barbara told me a story that took place back in the early 1990s, long before the internet and the ways social media keep us in a sort of instantaneous sense of contact. In fact, it was during these years that Barbara found herself back in contact with a love from twenty years prior. They were enjoying a correspondence with letters, something that only people of a certain generation will probably remember. Barbara and this man were not in close proximity. She lived in Ontario, Canada, and he was working as a middle school teacher in New Hampshire.

After some months had passed without a return letter from him, Barbara picked up the phone, called the school where he worked, and asked to speak with him. The school receptionist who took the call was sorry to have to explain that this man had passed away quite suddenly at the age of thirty-two from a brain aneurysm. Barbara was, of course, devastated by this shocking news, and truly found herself in a position of being emotionally unable to process it. She was blindsided by the news itself, but also this was long before cell phones, internet, and social media, so she was unable to find out anything about what had happened. She could not process the loss by exploring the details of how he had passed, what his health had been prior to the aneurysm, and all the unanswered questions that come when people die and we want the comfort of information.

While Barbara was still in this deep struggle, she had a dream one early morning. The dream took place in the very room in which she was sleeping, which is one of the standard ways that such visitation dreams are structured. She felt a presence in the room, and within the dream itself, she opened her eyes. There was her man, standing beside her bed, dressed as he had appeared in the 1970s when their relationship first formed. She had a sense that he appeared at this age and in that garb so that she would more easily recognize him. The details were very specific: backpack on his back, long hair, and the same type of clothing he preferred back then. And typical of such visitation dreams, he said to her, "I want to let you know that I'm okay and that I'm sorry you had to find out in the shocking way you did that I had died. Here I am. I'm well and happy." To this day, Barbara is not entirely sure what this experience was. Was it a dream? A soul coming to visit her? Truly, we'll never know for sure, but this is another of many such remarkable experiences, which are almost always life-changing and transformative.

Carri's husband of almost sixteen years died unexpectedly in the fall of 2018. They were separated at the time, and she described him as a difficult man presenting her with a difficult marriage. A few months after he passed, her husband came to her in a dream under the influence of a full moon. She described this as more of an experience than a dream, which by now you should recognize as a prominent feature of visitation dreams. She could feel him with her as clear as if he had been standing right in front of her in waking life. Placing his ethereal hands on her dream shoulders, he spoke intently to her, saying, "Carri, I am coming back. You need to look for me! Do you understand? I am healed and I am coming back. You need to look for me! Do you understand?" He said it over and over until finally she said, "Yes, I understand." Then he was gone.

Though her husband has reached out to her in other ways that Carri's intuition has provided access to, he has never again come to her in her dreams. And now we wait for him to indeed return. Will he? What does that even mean? Such is the mystery of this phenomenon that, when experienced, is as real for the dreamer as anything corporeal. At the end of the day, we'll never really know for sure. And perhaps the thing we know about least is why some people who have passed away will visit the loved ones who are still here in life. If there is one thing about visitation dreams that I have a lot of experience with, it is, unfortunately, that this experience cannot be ordered up, like something that might be delivered to you upon request. Over the years, so many people who are grieving the loss of a loved one have expressed to me deep sadness that their beloved has not visited them in the dream state.

We don't get to control this.

There is a belief that might be applicable here, something I have heard in spiritual spaces, that says a visitation will not occur if there isn't something that the souls need to work out between them—meaning that a visitation will happen only if there is a compelling need for either the departing soul or the one who is left experiencing the grief of death. I could not possibly speak to such a profound mystery, but I certainly have sat with many a distraught person suffering from a deep loss, longing for a connection in the dream state in the form of a visitation. The world of psychology would seek to dismiss the mystical elements of such dreams as merely a coping mechanism to help the process of grieving. The mystics have always been one step ahead of the scientists, and while you cannot insist that a loved one who has passed visit you in a dream, when it happens, it can be one of the most profound experiences some dreamers have ever had.

Chapter Six

Night Terrors and Multidimensionality

Welcome to the fascinating and complex world of night terrors. There is a phenomenon that is a part of the experience that is profoundly mystical in nature, and connects to a number of experiences that are perhaps the most outrageous things that can happen while we are asleep.

In order to truly understand some of these powerful, multidimensional experiences, we must start with the brain itself. Let's move through a little lesson in brain function and all the complexities of the sleep cycle, with an emphasis on the extraordinary things that take place during REM sleep. Yes, the eyes will move back and forth quite enthusiastically during this portion of sleep, hence the moniker *rapid eye movement*. This simple eye movement truly belies the complex series of actions that are taking place in the brain during REM sleep. In fact, some of the phenomena that we are diving into here are possible because of the relationship between the brain, the body, and therefore consciousness itself when we drop into this peak moment in the sleep cycle, and it all starts with brain waves.

REM sleep is not only the part of the cycle with the most vivid dream experiences, but also is where short-term memory is formed. Additionally, during REM sleep, we are cleaning out the metabolic waste that is discharged into the brain each day, because the separation of the brain from the rest of the body through the blood brain barrier requires the brain to flush its own toilet in a manner that is completely different from the rest of the body beyond that barrier. The neofrontal cortex, a portion of the brain that is quiet during the first five waves of sleep, lights up again, and the brain has a very clever way of protecting us from that activity, which is also part of the setup to the mystical experiences available just before and after REM sleep. Let's break all of this down, starting with sleep stages.

When we are awake, our brain lights up with brilliant amounts of energy that expresses in tremendous chaos and activity that we call waking consciousness. There are billions of neurons firing as we go about our day, doing things and receiving information from our environment about who, where, and when we are operating. Then we run out of steam, prepare to rest and restore, and find ourselves in bed, allowing the sweet death of sleep to overtake our embodiment. If you were measuring brain activity during the process of falling into sleep, you would see the initial chaos of wakefulness followed by a slowing down and elongating process. The waves of energy that seem static and disparate begin to coalesce into smoother waves, as measured by a sensitive instrument. The waves begin to appear to synchronize, and you can think of each of the first three stages of sleep as simply three successive levels that, as you descend through them, become slower and more synchronized.

After about ninety minutes of this, we get ready to drop into the REM cycle, and this is where it gets kind of crazy. The first process is initiated by inducing a paralysis of the body. This occurs because the very next step in the process is that the neofrontal cortex is going to light up, as excitedly as it is during wakefulness. Though our scientific understanding of all that is going on during REM is limited, we do know that it is during this cycle of sleep that experiences we have are turned into short- and long-term memory, and the extraneous material is discarded into the abyss of our unconscious. Imagine if you remembered every single thing your brain recorded each day. The sheer volume of data would overwhelm you. The brain does something truly miraculous. On a quantum level, we examine every impulse of the day before our last sleep, and sift through that tremendous amount of material to take the important information and add it to the narrative of our unfolding life.

This sleep paralysis is truly for our own protection, for without it, the body would respond to what the brain is lighting up. To put it simply, it works like this. When we are awake, the brain is all fired up as we move through the day operating our body and living our life. When we go to sleep, the brain quiets down, so much so that we experience a radically altered state that we call sleep. Once we hit that all-important moment of REM, our brain starts to act exactly as it does when we are wide awake. We have this way of shutting that down by the brain telling the body that it can't and shouldn't move. If we happen to wake up just a little while this process is going on, we have this frightening experience we call a night terror.

The body is turned off for a short period of time while the brain turns itself on full tilt. The eye movement during this cycle is inspired by the stimulation of the brain, and the images that the brain is reexperiencing show up as the physical behavior of the eyes darting about in their sockets. Without sleep paralysis, that same activity would translate directly into movement, so if someone's mechanism for this paralysis is insufficient, that person might move about their space while actually dreaming. We call this *somnambulism*, or sleepwalking. While this is not a chapter about sleepwalking, I trust that this perspective will help illustrate how blurry the lines are between consciousness, the unconscious, wakeful consciousness, sleeping consciousness, and the body, which does its best to contain all of these different levels of awareness.

When all is working well, however, the brain does what it does and the process completes itself. The sleep cycle advances to the next stage of deep sleep, the paralysis gently loosens its grip, and we usually rise up close to wakefulness before starting the entire process all over again, on average of three to four times a night. This process doesn't always work smoothly, and sometimes the sleep stage ends and the person begins to rise up in the direction of wakeful, conscious awareness, but only a little. This happens before the cycle is over, so the paralysis of the body is still in place. The person in the bed is indeed sleeping, but they have an awareness that they are in a dream. There is this tiny sliver of awareness that is now peeking into the experience, very much in the same manner as described in the chapter on lucid dreaming (chapter 2), only the body is still paralyzed, because technically the cycle is not over. This crisscrossing of signals sets up one of the most powerful sleeping and dreaming phenomena there is: night terrors.

Night terrors is the term for this experience of being in between the dream state and the waking state. In fact, it might be an important distinction that even though sleep paralysis is directly related to REM sleep, night terrors are not. This dysregulation between the brain and the body happens after REM, while the sleeper is in the deep sleep stage that happens right after REM but before wakefulness, and can occur after any of the several sleep cycles we go through every night. The dreamer is still very much asleep, so the felt experience is of being in a dream. There is conscious awareness, and often that includes understanding that this experience is happening in the very bed in which the person is sleeping.

In fact, there are lots of reports of people who suffer from night terrors on a regular basis who have trained themselves to wake up. Remember, this is still a dream state, so this awareness of the room does not feel the same as waking life, but very much like a dream. If this is a regularly occurring phenomenon, the dreamer has some conscious awareness of the state while they are in it. Forcing a little physical movement with great concentration of mind often wakes the person up fully enough to slough off the paralysis and move into the waking state. Of course, if there is not this awareness, then the half-asleep paralyzed state that is being forced onto the body can result in a sensation of pure terror for the dreamer.

These states have big names, like *hypnagogic* or *hypnopompic* hallucinations. The different monikers relate to whether this misalignment of sleep stages takes place at the beginning (hyp-nagogic) or the end (hypnopompic) of the sleep cycle. These distinctions are not as relevant to the dreamer who is having the night terror because the felt sensation is the same, whether it is being triggered before REM begins or after it ends. Either way, this crisscrossing of states generates a truly frightening experi-ence. This can happen so frequently for some people that it oper-ates at a level we would call a sleep disorder, and those people are in true suffering. There are medications that can help, but when someone has night terrors in this consistent manner, it can interfere with life and functioning in a big way. Outside of night terrors as a somewhat rare sleep disorder, this experience is com-mon enough that most human beings have experienced it at least once.

Night terrors are much more common in children and are often outgrown, but clearly this phenomenon is the origin of the boogeyman and those monsters that hide under the bed and behind the closet door. The reason that children have more night terrors than adults and often grow out of them is still a mystery. Certainly, children's brains are not fully formed, and in fact, it is typically not until a child is eight or nine years old that they can work with abstract reasoning, where overlapping and contradictory thoughts can exist at the same time: "I am in my bed, can't move, feel terrified, but wake up and know it was just a dream." The felt sensation and the reality as we know it contradict each other, but with abstract reasoning, we can work through those contradictions to create a full picture of something we are experiencing. A young child just thinks, "I had a scary dream." The young child's brain cannot put such contradictory thoughts together, so the fear, plus the empty room, puts the scary creature out of sight, under the bed or in the closet.

Things Do Go Bump in the Night!

When Yeraldi was in elementary school, she began having experiences of being in a terrifying dream that seemed to be taking place right in her bedroom, although she was still actually asleep and dreaming. The dream was that she would look up and see a person standing in front of the door to her bedroom. Well, *see* is a relative term here, because truly, the bedroom was dark, and although she could see this person's face, their body was challenging to make out in the dim light because they appeared to be wearing all black, including what seemed like black cloth draped around their body, topped with a black hat.

This was clearly a shadow dream, where the image of a specter in all black is symbolic of the archetype that lives inside of us all, the shadow as an archetypal figure. Jung postulated that we all have this as part of our essential makeup, an aspect of self that reflects an absence of life force and joy. Interestingly, the two additional shadow symbols of a hat, which might express dark thoughts, and a cloth, suggesting being enveloped by darker material as a form of outward expression, are both removable, suggesting that there might be some light underneath all that shadow.

The essence of the experience wasn't so much about the dark, ominous figure in front of Yeraldi's door. The thing that turned this into something terrifying was the feeling of immobility. Yeraldi felt paralyzed in these moments, and the frightening avatar in the room was directly connected to feeling unable to move her body while perceiving this scary being in front of her bedroom door. The experience intensified during her high school years, and she even began to recognize a strange falling sensation and a whooshing noise in her ears that signaled the sleep paralysis was taking over. Interestingly, both the feeling of being unable to move as well as the falling sensations are both dream symbols that represent our relationship to control. Being unable to move in a dream is expressing a lack of agency, and falling is a standard image that symbolizes feeling out of control. Both of these are frightening aspects of being human and add to the night terror's scary sensibility.

Natasha also had her first experience of what the doctors referred to as night terrors when she was a child. Hers were frequent enough that she was put on a medication that was designed to help her sleep deeply without dreaming, but it had side effects that caused the family to decide to discontinue its use. Like Yeraldi, Natasha would dream in a way that felt like she was awake but not really. She would see shadow figures in her room, including one dream that was specific and recurring where a shadow person would be in the corner of her room, but outside the window Natasha could see a huge fire and smoke. The silhouettes of little hands would bang on the window, screaming and crying to be heard.

Kirsty was in her early fifties at the time of this writing, but she still has vivid memories of night terrors that happened when she was around seven years old. It always began with her lying in bed on her back, with her eyes fixed on the glow of her parents' bedside light, which, because of the construction of their home, she could see through her bedroom window. Kirsty dreaded that light going out, as it left her in blackness that was terrifying to her. She would lie in bed in this state for what felt like hours, just staring into the dark and feeling utterly alone in the world. Being in the remote Australian Outback took the darkness of night and added natural but scary noises from outside in nature. This may sound like a story about a young girl afraid of the dark, but she also describes feeling that her eyes were clamped open, she could not move, and nobody was coming to help. This last piece—not being able to move—is what tells us she was not just lying in bed awake all night afraid of the dark, but was, in fact, suffering from one of the most potentially terrifying things that can happen within the world of dreams.

Demonic Figures in Dreams

Night terrors have had a hand in creating ideas that have become stuck in the human psyche. The idea of the bogeyman, that terrifying entity that lives beneath the bed or behind the closet door of children all over the world, is a perfect example of a demonic creature that has its origins in complex dream experiences. The term *succubus* is an alteration of the Latin *succuba*, or "paramour," from *succubāre*, "to lie under." English usage of this word dates back to the late fourteenth century, but there is plenty of evidence that this notion is not exclusively Judeo-Christian. In Jewish mysticism, the succubus is a primary archetype, and Adam's first wife, Lilith, was cast as a succubus after leaving him and refusing the return to the Garden of

Eden to live in subservience to him. Lilith's story was removed as an origin story, and the subservient version of women was depicted in the story of Eve being created from Adam's rib. Lilith was cast out and later interpreted as a sexual deviant and one of the true original succubi.

Even Buddhist canon has evidence of this archetype through a powerful prayer that promises that those who drop into this prayer will be protected from attack by demons who suck your energy or make love to you in your dreams. Arabic mythology has its own spirit similar to the succubus that goes by the name *Qarinah*. This image, too, reflects a nefarious spiritual energy that shares the sleeping space with men and will often generate what is reported as a spiritual attack on them that happens during sleep, with an emphasis on sexual content.

Our modern sense of these demonic forces really originated in the period of time typically referred to as the Dark Ages, where religion was dominant and superstitions became the spiritual laws of the day. The strict dogma being imposed on undereducated populations generated superstitions and fears that were easily projected onto sexuality as something to be ashamed of and a rejection of women as powerful healers connected to ancient wisdom. These demons were inventions of the Church, which used such superstitions to control people.

Images of the succubus and incubus (a male evil spirit who is believed to have sex with women while they are sleeping) show up across cultures and throughout history. There may be a component of religiosity involved in the perpetuation of such myths, certainly in Christianity, where dogmatic morals were reinforced by frightening images of the dangers of too much sexual freedom. The ubiquity of these figures in different cultures certainly suggests that there may be some actual phenomena associated with the rise of such imagery.

I had an experience with a young man in the early 2000s who explained to me that he had been someone who suffered from night terrors, but had completely transformed his experience. My curiosity piqued, I asked him if he might sit with me to describe what his journey had been like. His story was grounded in a lifelong experience of night terrors. They began in childhood, as they often do. Many children outgrow this experience, but this young man did not. The adult experience of night terrors can be so persistent that it is considered a sleep disorder, which can be very problematic and cause all sorts of ancillary challenges that come from constant interrupted sleep. This man did not have night terrors at the level of a sleep disorder, but they were frequent enough that he considered them a routine part of his day-to-day life.

Typical of all night terror experiences, this man would rouse a bit in his sleeping consciousness just enough to have the experience of being in full sleep, solidly in REM stage, but also with a conscious perception of immobility due to the brain paralyzing the body. He would feel like he was dreaming, but also be fully aware of being in the bed he was in, so the dream was telling him that he was dreaming of lying in his own bed. Then the awareness of his inability to move would bleed into that dream experience, and he would feel the panic and terror that gives this experience its name. This young man had an instinct that rose up in him that he could not explain but was unshakable. He felt that this experience could be transformed if he put some attention on what he was experiencing while he was experiencing it.

One of the things that impressed me about this young man was that he had no knowledge of the state he found himself in in his sleep patterns. Without any outside information to inform him, his internal guidance took over, and this is how he described what he did in a process that he reported took about three months to unfold. He started by simply attempting to relax when the awareness of the terror rose up. He explained that this was incredibly uncomfortable, but he would use his thoughts to encourage himself to somehow relax and stay present, no matter how frightened he felt. After a few weeks of this, he was able to be more fully present to what he was experiencing in the room, and though he still felt unable to move, eventually the fear that the sensation was generating left his thoughts.

After some weeks, what happened was a figure began to form in his mind's eye, but in manner where the young man was fully aware that what he was perceiving was an actual energetic presence. It had structure and a kind of form, though again it was, at this point, just an idea in his imagination. But this was no ordinary waking-life fantasy. He could tell with some certainty that what he was beginning to see with his inner vision and feel with his body was a literal entity, separate from him but sitting right on top of his chest. The form of this entity was dark and truly frightening. By the time he got to this point in his process, he was easily managing his fear through his focused thoughts and weeks of practice.

Now what happened next opened my eyes to something tremendous that I have been in deep consideration of ever since, and this entire chapter and my thoughts about such experiences originated in this part of this young man's narrative. Gradually, in a process that took a few weeks to play out, the fear began to subside. The young man eventually had enough mornings where, though the fear would rise up from the sensation that he could not move or breathe, he developed an ease with the uncomfortable feelings, because he transcended the lower, fearful thoughts of being in danger. The immobility was not dangerous, and though the sensation of not being able to breathe had begun as a perceived fact, the actual truth was that he could breathe just fine. In a process that was ultimately meditative, he found that by releasing the layers of fear and discomfort, the vision he was having began to change dramatically.

Slowly, day by day, a visual emerged in his mind's eye of a white light, a beautiful feminine energy that was indeed interacting with him in a sexual manner. What started out as a glimpse became a full-on perceptive experience of what he described as an almost impossibly beautiful being of light that felt feminine in nature to him. His early morning natural arousal and this energetic experience that was also deeply erotic developed into what became a beautiful and satisfying experience that had started out as pure terror. By being willing to lean into that fear, he was able to transcend the illusions of what was happening, and his inner eye opened up wide to a multidimensional experience that was truly mind-blowing to him and, in the telling of this tale, to me as well.

Remember Natasha from earlier in this chapter, whose night terrors began in childhood? While many people have night terrors as children, a good deal of them grow out of the experience and do not continue to have them as adults. But this was not the case with Natasha, and she also shared with me a night terror experience she had just a few years before this book was written.

> I was asleep with my partner, but I "woke up." I saw this thing enter through our office doorway that connects to our bedroom. It was a smoky white tall and long figure. I felt panic and tightness take over my whole body. I wanted to wake up my other half, but couldn't move or talk. The thing got closer and closer until it was finally beside me on my bed, the blank black eyes just staring at me. I still couldn't move. It reached its unusually long, thin hand toward me and placed one finger on my abdomen. I got a sharp, horrible pain and finally was able to move. I shot right up in bed crying in pain, waking up my partner, and the thing was gone.

Now just because this type of dream falls in a distinct category of experience does not mean there is no room for interpretation. If we take out the nefarious feelings that the paralysis engendered in Natasha, we have a dream where a higher-consciousness energy was indicating that something about Natasha's abdomen was expressing some form of negative feedback. And, in fact, when she finally broke free of the grip of the dreamlike paralysis, she felt something wet down around her legs, and when she checked, it was blood. She and her partner went to the hospital and learned that she had been, unbeknownst to either of them, pregnant, and during the night she had miscarried. Some people might be tempted to fall prey to the scary feelings that accompany these experiences and declare that the dark figure caused the miscarriage.

Natasha is someone who has a deep spiritual connection and routinely communicates with spirits and other entities both in her waking life and at times in her sleep. I firmly believe, as I have attempted to outline in this chapter, that the frightening sensations of night terrors come from the paralysis, and that if we could remove that quality from her experience, we would see that the guide that came and pointed to her abdomen was likely a higher-consciousness aspect of her and not some dark outside force who came to end a pregnancy.

Chapter Seven

Dreams of Inspiration and Problem-Solving

I'm going to sleep on it. This innocuous phrase has come to mean something akin to "I'll think about that tomorrow." But, in fact, sleeping on it has much more depth and power than might be apparent in the simplicity of the suggestion. The dream state is a profound place of problem-solving and inspiration, and history is filled with examples of stories where guidance came through the dreams of individuals who ended up changing the course of history.

I can still remember being introduced to the periodic table of elements in the early weeks of my high school physics class. I was already steeped in my fascination with dreams, and it was during these years that I first began listening to the dreams of my high school compatriots and offering interpretations in an intuitive way. Anything that involved the world of dreams or dream interpretation pricked up my ears. For those of you who need a little reminder of what the periodic table of elements is, it is a chart that assembles all of the known elements in order of atomic number horizontally and in specific groupings of like acting elements vertically.

It turns out that there is an elegant and stunning natural organization to these elements. The human being who discovered and codified this very specific and ordered structure was Siberian-born chemist Dmitri Mendeleev. His discovery took the world by storm and changed forever how we relate to the elements that make up our universe. Mendeleev's waking mind was vigorously occupied with the quest for a classification system that would order the elements. The dream he had, of course, was just a function of what the human brain normally does during sleep—organizing and consolidating the ideas, images, and bits of information that occupy our waking hours.

Dmitri Mendeleev described how he could feel the formation of this structure in his head, but found himself unable to bridge the gap between inner, intuitive understanding and an outer mode of expression that would allow what he was grasping to be presented to others. The dream he had fulfilled the function of typical dreaming that all human beings experience, where the dreamer's nighttime fixation is directly related to the daytime perseverations of the dreamer's mind. We all work out our problems in this unconscious way, though for Mendeleev, one particular dream would help him transform the world. He wrote in his diary the morning after this dream, "I saw in a dream a table where all the elements fell into place as required.

Awakening, I immediately wrote it down on a piece of paper."
And the rest is, as they say, history.[1]

A more modern example of problem-solving in dreams
comes to us from Silicon Valley, where uber-nerd Larry Page
came up with the idea for Google in his dream state. When he
was a graduate student in the 1990s, Page feared that a clerical
mistake had led to his acceptance to Stanford University. Due to
this irrational fear, Page dreamt one night of downloading and
storing the internet on individual computers. Soon after waking up, Page did some simple calculations and concluded that
while that particular goal wasn't possible, he was able to create a searchable database of links to web pages. This is how he
described his experience in an interview.

> I want to talk about dreams for a second. And in my case,
> literally a dream. When I was in college, I was sure that I
> had been admitted [to Stanford] by a clerical error, prob-
> ably a computer error. And because of that I had an irra-
> tional fear I'd be sent home on the bus. ... But it turns out,
> because of that anxiety, I woke up literally with a dream.
> And it was kind of a strange dream. It went like, "I think I
> could download the entire web onto small computers that
> were lying around." And that would probably seem pretty
> crazy to most people, but I stayed up a couple hours in the
> middle of the night, doing some math, and it seemed actu-
> ally pretty plausible, while assuming you actually didn't

---

1. Maria Popova, "How Mendeleev Invented His Periodic Table in a Dream,"
The Marginalian, accessed October 2023, https://www.themarginalian.org
/2016/02/08/mendeleev-periodic-table-dream/. Original quotation appears
in Paul Strathern's *Mendeleyev's Dream* (New York: Hamish Hamilton, 2000).

keep any of the web pages, you only kept the links. And then I sort of figured out, given all that data, I thought it would take a couple weeks. And I told my advisor that, and he just sort of laughed at me. And of course it took a year or two, but at the end of that, we had a way to rank web pages and no thoughts to search at all, and eventually search entered the picture, and you know the rest and that became Google. ... So I'd like to encourage everyone to follow their dreams.[2]

Good advice, Mr. Page. In fact, in the 1960s, the Rolling Stones let us know how challenging life can be with their hit song "(I Can't Get No) Satisfaction," in what would be an anthem for baby boomers. Keith Richards followed his dreams one morning, on May 7, 1965, to be exact. Mr. Richards reportedly woke up in the early morning hours from a dream, grabbed a tape recorder, and laid down the opening riff of this song, then promptly fell back asleep. But there it was, a gift that came directly from his unconscious, which he then tweaked a bit, and it became a gift he shared with the world.[3]

There is a tale about Thomas Edison, who is famous for eschewing sleep, preferring only about four hours of formal bedtime each day in exchange for a work life that captivated his attention. He was fond of naps, but apparently not for the

2. "Google's Secret—Larry Page Interview," 20 Percent channel, September 5, 2020, YouTube video, 1:03–2:33, https://www.youtube.com/watch?v =X0pEa8gjH1Y.

3. "'Satisfaction' Comes to Keith Richards in His Sleep," History.com, last updated May 5, 2020, https://www.history.com/this-day-in-history/satisfaction-comes -to-keith-richards.

restorative function of the act. When he was facing a daunting problem, he would hold two balls, one in each hand. As he dozed off, he would inevitably drop one of the balls, which would trigger him immediately into wakefulness. The stage-one sleep state that he would drop into, though not a full sleep cycle, as he might have experienced during his paltry four hours a night in bed, allowed his conscious mind to begin to slip away and dip into an in-between state known as hypnagogic, which you learned all about in the previous chapter. The hypnagogic state is rich with inner perceptions, and Mr. Edison believed that by napping in this manner, he was potentially dipping into a space in his consciousness that offered inspiration and ideas that came from a different place than his waking consciousness.[4]

Now, not all of us are going to discover a universal law of physics or invent a life-changing technology, but we too can have profound experiences of solving problems through the dream state. We don't have to passively wait around for a dream to drop into our lap, helping us solve problems. Our waking life is pure conscious awareness. In sleep and dreams, we are dropped fully into the unconscious mind, the arguably much larger element of our humanity that contains all the information we could ever need to have a meaningful life driven by self-awareness. There is a powerful technique in dreamwork where you ask your dreams to inform you of what your unconscious has to say about a particular challenge you are moving

4. Brian Roemmele, "Thomas Edison's Secret Trick to Maximize His Creativity by Falling Asleep," HuffPost, October 28, 2017, https://www.huffpost.com /entry/thomas-edisons-secret-trick-to-maximize-his-creativity_b_59f4d276 e4b06ae9067ab91c

through. There are many ways to refer to this engagement, but my go-to terminology is *petitioning your dreams.* This is a process where you pose a question in your waking life and ask your dreams to bring you guidance, wisdom, or information about a particular struggle or problem you are having in your waking life.

Of the many things that Jung said about dreams, he once wrote that "dreams may contain ineluctable truths, philosophical pronouncements, illusions, wild fantasies, memories, plans, anticipations, irrational experiences, even telepathic visions, and heaven knows what besides."[5] Our conscious awareness may be the aspect of our human experience that is fully available to us as we move through life, but the unconscious is the much greater aspect of the self, and when we learn how to interpret unconscious material in our daily, waking life, we have a much more powerful setup for self-investigation and growth. One could argue that the desire we have to know and understand ourselves demands that we have some sort of relationship with the part of us that we can't touch directly, but that on some level knows everything about who we are and why we do what we do.

I first learned about the technique of petitioning dreams when I was a young man in my twenties and was learning all I could about dreamwork, outside of my own organic relationship to dreams and dream interpretation that I had developed in my adolescence and into early adulthood. I was taking a workshop about dreams and learned about a process that I

---

5. C. G. Jung, "The Practical Use of Dream-Analysis," in *Practice of Psychotherapy*, vol. 16 of *The Collected Works of C. G. Jung*, edited and translated by Gerhard Adler and R. F. C. Hull, 2nd ed. (Princeton, NJ: Princeton University Press: 1966), 317. Originally published in 1934.

have used ever since in my own practice. It has also become one of my go-to techniques when working with others who wish to dive more deeply into their self-actualization journey. This technique is an effective way to work with your unconscious and make more powerful decisions for yourself as you move through life.

I'm going to illustrate the technique of petitioning a dream for you first by describing an experience I had in the last decade of my own journey. This process is often not clear and precise, and one of the tricks to working well with the tenuous bridge between the conscious and unconscious minds is to trust that the unconscious has the reins. Our job is not to understand what is unconscious, because that is actually not possible. What is unconscious is truly unconscious, and will always remain so. What we can do, however, which is a process that is lifelong and not just relegated to this type of work, is learn to interpret our unconscious patterns while we watch them play out in our daily lives.

With every year that passes, we grow in age and wisdom. The more self-actualized we are, the more we understand how to look at our behaviors and the things that are happening in our lives as direct reflections of our unconscious. When we can spot the moments of conflict, negation, fear, and holding back, we have a much easier time facing our demons, understanding the lesson of the moment, and coming out the other side with greater self-awareness.

This experience happened only about ten years ago at the close of an extended period of abstinence, where I was not dating or exploring relationship, and I had not had sex with anyone in over six years. I could feel that it was time to begin turning outward and to explore intimacy with others, and I began to open myself up to dating once again. I was fifty years old at the time, so I was no stranger to the ways that my childhood relationships with my parents had impacted my relationships with the various men I had been intimately involved with in my life. This is how relationships work, in fact, and if there are wounds to heal based on those early childhood experiences, you will attract the people into your life who are perfectly designed to help you confront emotional patterns and heal them through what happens in an intimate relationship in a life lived consciously. Sometimes these patterns are still loosely in place but just need a little jolt from the unconscious to alert us to how they are playing out at a given time.

At that time, I met a man who I dated for a number of months. There was enough curiosity and chemistry to keep me engaged for a time, but it wasn't long before I had a sense that something was not right, and I began to feel ambivalent about staying in this experience. At the same time, there was this yummy chemistry, and I was excited at the prospect of exploring relationship again after a rather long hiatus. Eventually the conflict grew, and so did the ambivalence, and I turned to dreamwork, specifically petitioning my dreams for some guidance. I knew what my conscious mind was thinking about this connection, but I needed to know what my unconscious had to offer.

One evening, I did the things you will hear me describe a number of times in this chapter. First, I made sure to treat my transition from my day to preparing for sleep with a little more energetic respect than I might on a typical night. Remember what we learned in chapter 6 about all the processes that occur during REM sleep, and understand that if you bombard your mind with a plethora of images right before going to bed, your brain will have to process all that detritus in the dream state. By limiting what you take in during those last hours before sleep, you are decreasing the amount of work your brain will have to do sifting through all that stimulation, so your unconscious can get to the business of expressing the unconscious more directly, fully, and efficiently.

The next step in the process is to set an intention. I have been doing this sort of work for three decades, so I operate in a place relative to my own consciousness where this is automatic for me. If I want a dream to offer me an answer to a question, I simply ask. While in that liminal state that comes between turning off the light and beginning to drop into sleep, I will ask myself to bring a dream to address a particular struggle I am having. This is a muscle that has been strengthened by over three decades of this sort of work. If you are just beginning this type of dreamwork, the more structured and specific you can be with the intention-setting process, the better. One of the most powerful ways to codify any intention is to write it down.

You might even consider writing your intention as a letter to your higher self. Some people like to refer to this higher consciousness as the dreaming self. You could also use any name that is comfortable for you to address multidimensional realms, such as Great Spirit, Holy Spirit, or God. Using the dreamwork standard of Dreaming Self, I might write something like this:

Dear Dreaming Self,

I am struggling with ambivalence about the dating experience I am having with Alex. Please bring a dream to help illuminate what my unconscious would have me know about this question at this time. For only the highest good, I allow myself to receive this guidance.

Sincerely,
Michael

This example is not presented as a literal template, for there is no right way to do this. Intention is everything, and for many people, putting pen to paper will concretize the desire and the request. What doing it as a letter accomplishes is to sort of target the desire where you want it. The notion of a higher self is vast and overwhelming, so formulating the request as a letter brings the implication that you know where in the unconscious this request is being directed. You don't really, but the unconscious doesn't know that, so the power of the letter will direct the intention right where it needs to land.

Here's the dream that followed. I was at an event of some sort. It felt like a celebration, complete with tables, guests, catered food, and lots of friends gathered around me. I understood this to be a celebration of my and my partner's anniversary of some sort, as I was married in this dream. In the first scene, I was in the space where the crowd was gathered, and my partner was in the other room. I felt a kind of irony in that, as the celebration was for the relationship I was in, but privately I knew that this relationship was over. I wanted out and had made the decision in my mind to end it. What was key in the dream was that I was the only one who knew of my intentions. Neither my partner nor any of our guests were aware of my unhappiness and the decision that had come out of it. There was also the knowing that my partner had been behaving badly at this event, which added to my consternation. After a moment, he entered the main room and came up to me. I was astonished to see that it was my father. Needless to say, I was both gobsmacked and amused by this. Indeed, this relationship was straight out of the past, a template of the kinds of attractions that had not turned into satisfying intimate connections because they had been generated from past wounds. I had outgrown this pattern, and within a few days I ended the relationship.

The challenge with this work is trusting the answer you receive, no matter what. My story, and the other stories I will share in this chapter, are examples of where the resulting dream yielded a clear sense of unconscious information. This process can be both fun and sometimes alarming in its precision, but we are dealing with the realm of ultimate mystery with the unconscious, so there will be many times when the dream that comes may not draw a clear and straight line between petition and response. Sometimes you will ask for guidance and wake up the next morning without any dream memory. Having faith in the unconscious is imperative here, and you must trust the answer, even when it doesn't make perfect sense.

Trusting the process can be difficult, especially when you read about a whole bunch of clear examples in this chapter. Remember that your unconscious mind is in constant conversation with your conscious awareness, and this is what happens each night when you sleep and dream. So even just writing down and ruminating over a dream that comes after a specific petition will stir up this ongoing interaction. Just know that more may be revealed in the course of the day, as well as in future dreams. This is the same approach to take on mornings that yield no dream memory after asking for an answer.

Tell Me Something True and I Will Believe You

In my search for dreamers' stories about this technique of petitioning a dream, it seems that relationship conflict is a common motivation for many people. Of the many stories I received, more of them were about relationship challenges that people found guidance for through their dreams than any other topic.

A Canadian woman named Loretta was visiting Glastonbury, England, at a time when she was dating a man who is now her husband, which may clue you in as to how this dream petition played out. At the time of this trip, they were in the early throws of their relationship, and they were both questioning their future. He had taken a job in the United States, and our dreamer moved in with her parents while he was away for work. Their many talks about their relationship led to a decision to consciously take some time for consideration and regroup after a time. This was partly what inspired Loretta to take a trip that was, essentially, a spiritual quest to a place known for its high vibration.

While on this trip, Loretta went to bed one evening and specifically asked for guidance in the form of a prayer, asking her higher self to reveal what she truly wanted. She trusted that her dreams would bring her an answer, and they did not disappoint. Her dream that night was of being in a horrible accident, after which her husband was pulled from the wreckage, badly bruised and bleeding. He was taken away on a gurney, and the fear and sadness that rose up in the dream was overwhelming. As she held his hand, she screamed, "Don't leave! I'm here. I love you so much." Loretta woke up crying, as the emotional content of the dream followed her into her morning. Here is what she had to say about her experience of this dream and what it led to:

> I woke up crying. I knew immediately that I wanted the relationship and did not want it to end. I thanked myself for showing me that I really did want the relationship and the effort I needed to put into it. I looked at my phone, and he had sent me some messages prior to him going to bed, and I felt a rush of love run over me. That day I went to the store, purchased a postcard, and declared my love for him in that card. Nine years later, we're still together. He joined me in Glastonbury five years after that, and we plan on going next year for my ten-year reunion trip. The intensity and vividness of the dream was deep. I honestly don't remember having another dream ever like it.

Dreamer Lynn loved her job at a bookstore, which she had to leave at the onset of the COVID-19 pandemic when such businesses were forced to close. As time passed, the bookstore offered the opportunity to return to a job she loved. Lynn was concerned about returning to the public retail space and wanted a dream to inform the decision at hand. Here is the dream that resulted, in her own words.

> I have returned to my bookstore job, and the dream takes place at a party given for all the "coolest" people working there. I know I am not cool, but I also know that I worked at this bookstore back in the day, before many of the current employees were even born! My "maturity," in this case, makes me an invitee. As I walk around the party, I don't see anyone I know, and the general mood of the party is one in which people are getting "wasted." I feel like an observer, curious, wondering what the draw is to a secret room in the back of the party house. I just know that that's where the COOLEST people have been invited to go, and I decide that I am cool enough to check it out.
>
> I find my way back into the secret coolest-of-the-cool-person room, and I see a guy who is considered the coolest guy of them all. He's in his mid-thirties, and I've only seen him from afar in the past. But then I see that there are people around him, sick and vomiting. He is MAKING THEM EAT HIS SHIT! I am shocked! I realize how awful the scene really is! My thoughts are racing, and I think to myself, "I better get out of here!" I see that the people in this secret room are very sad and yet willing to put up with the indignities. I leave the party and wake up.

Lynne described waking up with complete certainty that her time at the bookstore had officially ended, and she felt clear that she would now move on to better things. She even shared that in the months that followed, there were times when her mind would wonder about job openings at the bookstore, and simply recalling the smell of the dream would cause her to laugh and accept the dream's wisdom once again.

Here is an example that reflects powerful guidance from the dream state of a mother having challenges with a decision her adult daughter was making. This was not a direct question-and-answer situation. In fact, the response that the dream petition offered had our dreamer make a specific decision, and at first glance the guidance may have been interpreted to reflect a positive outcome for the daughter and her narrative. As you will see, the seemingly positive answer to this dream petition simply put the mother in close proximity to her daughter as she, the daughter, was about to fall off the proverbial cliff, and the mother was right there at the time she was most needed.

Jennifer was a woman in her sixties with an adult daughter who was one of six children. Jennifer had always been an avid dreamer and had enjoyed receiving insight from her dreams for many years. One of her daughters was an MIT-educated woman who, after completing an internship in Tel Aviv, was visiting Jordan on holiday. The young woman met a Bedouin tour guide there and began an intense relationship that generated eleven different visits, as the daughter fell madly in love and decided to marry this man. Because this was kept hidden from the family, Jennifer was surprised to learn that her daughter not only intended to marry this man, but had also spent enormous amounts of her own money to help him financially, investing in his business and even making large purchases for his benefit.

Needless to say, their were red flags all over this narrative. Jennifer had strong instincts that her daughter was in trouble, but she also had more than a small amount of guilt that she was not supporting something that was so important to one of her children. As she went to bed that night, she asked her dreaming self the following question: "Is it beneficial to accompany my daughter to Jordan?" That night, the following dream presented itself.

In my dream I was in a tourist information room looking at a map on the wall, a map of my neighborhood. In walked President John Kennedy. (I am 64, so I have a reference for his presidency.) He was wearing traveler's clothes, shorts, button-down casual shirt. He pointed a teacher's old-style wooden pointer stick on the map and said, "Go there." When I looked at the map, it was now the map of the world.

The dream response was pretty clear to Jennifer, and that morning she called her daughter and told her to go ahead and book the tickets. Clearly, the dream indicated that traveling was imminent, and she (Jennifer) responded to that. As you will see as this story continues to play out, the image of President Kennedy being the avatar in the dream has some interesting interpretive and intuitive data to offer.

Upon Jennifer's arrival in Jordan, it became very apparent that this man was both overly controlling and verbally abusive. In the moments in between these bouts, he could be exceedingly charming, evidence of a person with a narcissistic personality of some measure. Ironically, the wedding was postponed because of a technical glitch involving a missing document. During the two weeks of waiting, this man's true colors appeared clearly enough that even the daughter could no longer look upon her beloved with eyes closed. During this waiting period, a third party confirmed that this man had a history of swindling women out of money, so the writing was on the wall.

Here's where it gets interesting to me. Clearly, having her mother present allowed the daughter to see the circumstances objectively. After this two-week pause, the marriage did not occur, and mother and daughter returned home to the US, safe and sound. Now, the symbolism of the image of John F. Kennedy in the dream is interesting at a deeper level. Kennedy's persona as a heroic president was underpinned by a darker, more personal sense of hidden demons, as his infidelity and marital integrity belied his heroic persona. An aspirational figure whom Jennifer would absolutely trust was the one who showed up in her dream to inspire her to travel, but the underlying message of relationship abuse was also in the resulting dream, though it might have required the clearer vantage point gained after some time had passed to see this subtle shade of interpretation.

Nancy and LouAnne were close friends, so much so that Nancy referred to them as "sister close, like-minded and supportive of each other." They had a tremendous amount in common and loved to share their stories with each other, "the good, the bad, and the ugly," as Nancy expressed it to me. Their friendship had formed and blossomed while they both were living in Arizona, but life happens, and their respective paths took them to other places. Our dreamer Nancy relocated back to New Jersey, and her dear friend LouAnne went to Ohio to care for her mother. Their relationship became one supported by frequent phone calls, and when LouAnne got sick with lung cancer, the phone calls increased.

Then came the fated weekend when Nancy found herself calling LouAnne constantly but the phone remained unanswered. A call to LouAnne's daughter revealed what was happening. Normally a strong, stoic woman, the daughter broke down on the phone telling Nancy that LouAnne was in the hospital and had been told to get her affairs in order, as she had been given about a week to live. There was already a plan for a visit on the calendar, and Nancy was reluctant to change those plans, to which the daughter declared plaintively, "If you want to see my mother alive, come now." There were other complications around taking sudden time off from work to accommodate immediate and unexpected travel. Our dreamer politely told the daughter that she would sleep on it, but what she really meant was that she would petition her dreams for an answer.

That night, as Nancy went to bed, she asked God for a sign in her dreams indicating if she should go to Ohio now. An interesting thing to note here is the language of the petition. Early in the chapter, I outlined ways to codify this process, but for Nancy, the way to the guidance was through asking God. This is key: it is better to work with what feels organic to you than to use some language that you find in a book. For Nancy, asking God was the perfect way to trigger her unconscious to deliver the goods, and there was no reason at all to change the approach. Of course, God delivered beautifully with the following dream, which replicated what happened during the earlier phone call.

In the dream, a young woman walks toward Nancy, and as she gets closer, Nancy recognizes her as LouAnne's daughter. Standing directly in front Nancy, the young woman looks directly in her eyes and repeats the message from the phone call: "If you want to see my mother alive, come now." The same message in waking life did not have the same gravitas as this deeper message did. Feeling empowered by this dream, Nancy took the time off, despite her challenging new boss. She drove from New Jersey to Ohio and got to spend an entire day with her beloved friend. LouAnne died the next day, surrounded by her family and her friend who was almost a sister to her. The dream state, and her respect for the wisdom that comes from within, allowed Nancy to have a beautiful experience of closure that she would have otherwise missed.

Here's an interesting story about an avid dreamer, April, having a recurring dream as she was moving through a difficult decision related to her work and career. A woman in her fifties in a male-dominated industry, April tended to find herself consistently in leadership roles, which often brought an experience of what can happen when men are intimidated by a strong woman in work spaces. April was in a fairly high-paying job, and though she had a strong desire to leave, she was struggling with this choice, most notably due to fears that she would not be able to replicate the benefits of this job if she took the great risk of leaving.

Because April has a strong spiritual practice and a good connection to working with her dreams, she asked Spirit to offer guidance in the dream state about this decision she was facing. As soon as she triggered this process, a recurring dream rose up, and it kept coming while she was considering her options. This dream template was very literal. It contained all the people and players from the job, and each were performing the same roles in April's dream that they occupied in waking life. In each dream, certain group dynamics would unfold, with intentional plots and plans to keep April in a place of feeling undermined and stripped of her ability to lead.

The same theme played out in each of the recurring iterations of this dream, but at the end of each dream, someone would die. And though each dream offered a different individual to be sacrificed to this dream death, the message was becoming more and more clear. After months of addressing this waking-life struggle and the recurring nighttime dream message, April was able to come to a place where the truth of the situation was clear. She left the job and moved halfway across the country to begin the next chapter. Not surprisingly, the recurring dream stopped as soon as she left.

I came across a dream experience from a woman named Laura that could fit into a tale about petitioning dreams but is also a bit of a visitation dream. Laura had been struggling to choose a place to move to where she could truly feel at home in the next chapter of her life. She described not having a powerful sense of home, and was searching for someplace that would allow this desire to manifest in the best manner possible. At the time of our conversation, her husband was no longer alive. But in the ten years since his passing, she had come to consider him a soul guide, so she was not surprised that the dream in which she asked for guidance on where to move also included a visitation from her deceased spouse.

After a long day of researching potential locations, Laura decided to ask her dream life to assist her in this investigative process. In the dream that came, she was with her husband

and their now-adult children were still young, so the dream was harkening back to a consciousness of when their family was vibrant and in growth mode. The children were playing on the side while she and her husband sat at a table, discussing their options. They talked of several places, the pros and cons of each, but mostly as those locations might impact him with regard to his career in the military.

After a moment of pause in the dream, the husband declared that they were moving to South Carolina. What was interesting to Laura about this was the fact that this location was not on her list at all, and in waking life would not have actually been on her husband's radar, as the area did not have a military base. In the latter part of the dream, he began to outline the benefits of life in the mountains of western South Carolina, detailing specific things about it that she would love about living there. Laura woke up quite certain that she should move to South Carolina, and further research revealed a wonderful climate, culture, and topography. At the time of this writing, Laura had not wavered in her decision and was looking for land to purchase to start her next chapter.

Sam's problem was more of a desire and an intention and less of an actual challenge he was facing, and as such, it might fit into other chapters of this book as well. It was an intriguing story to me for this chapter, as it models the process of increasing intuitive and mystical connections through dreams and dreaming. Sam described to me his relationship with his own dreaming as something that "is always evolving and growing." He has had out-of-body experiences and has even practiced shared dreaming with one of his best friends. In one instance, both of them found that they had dreamed about a swimming pool. While this shared dream occurred, each was unaware that not only was the other person sleeping and having the same dream, but they were also both napping on their respective couches. We can tell from these experiences that Sam is a fairly avid dreamer, and his psyche opens up easily through the dream state.

Sam reported returning to his spiritual path after some periods of distraction in the years 2017 and 2018. Sam shared with me that "animals light me up, so much so that I also have quite a few animal tattoos." It was this combined love of animals and his burgeoning spirituality that led him to this exploration. Toward the end of this awakening process, he came upon a book that promised to teach him how to connect with the realm of power animals, a beautiful sort of medicine that can best be accessed through the dream state. The book was designed to teach people to connect, through their dreams, with power animal medicine. The practice was simple, and like most dreamwork, it was based on intention. Sam was simply instructed, during the powerful and fertile time as his mind was drifting off into sleep, to use what mental focus was left to work with a mantra, such as "Please let me meet my power animal," and to keep repeating this as he fell asleep.

In typical fashion, this technique did not net a result immediately, but on the third consistent night of asking, Sam was richly rewarded.

> During the night it felt as if I was stirring in bed and I was in between sleep and waking up when I had not one but four animal visions. The first to appear was a bear. The second

was a wolf. The third was an owl, and the fourth was a unicorn—yep, a bloody unicorn. Their appearances were like bright golden line drawings, and they were moving around. They didn't stay for long, but I sure remembered them when I woke up in the morning.

Sam drew some distinctions from these visions, including the following:

So what answers were my beautiful four beings helping and teaching me? Bear keeps me grounded and helps me connect to Mother Earth. Wolf reminds me to be empowered and love with an open heart. Owl teaches me not only that I already hold the wisdom I need but to help me see through the dark too. Unicorn guides me in my co-creation with Spirit, reminding me we are all one.

Truly, here is the thing that Sam said to me that rises to the top of what I want to express to you. Sam wrote, "If I can connect to my power animal guides, then so can anyone." And Sam is absolutely right about that.

Chapter Eight

Mystical Dream Downloads and Night School

There are dreams that fall into a category all their own and clearly don't have the same structure as the typical chaotic and mutable landscapes we find in more pedestrian dreams. These amplified and heightened experiences are a powerful way that humans connect to the spiritual and energetic realms, and they must be viewed differently. Before diving into the dream content I will share with you in this chapter, let's explore some things about energy, the brain, and our human capacity for heightened spiritual experiences.

There is a well-known concept of energy centers in the body known as *chakras*. From a modern spiritual perspective, there are seven main chakras, arranged from top to bottom in a row. The root chakra is grounded at the base of the spine. The next one up is known as the sacral chakra and is related to the reproductive organs. The solar plexus chakra is where we find our gut instincts and where we first connect to nurturance through the navel. The center one is the heart chakra because of, well, love. Communication is the focus of the throat chakra, the fifth one up from the bottom. The sixth chakra, known as the brow or third eye chakra, is in some ways the most important one for our purposes, because this is the seat of our intuition and where we receive divine guidance. The top chakra, the seventh, is known as the crown chakra and is where we connect with that divine energy that pours down on us from above.

Each of these energy centers correlates with physical structures in the body. For example, the root chakra is directly connected to the digestive power of the colon. The gonads are what make up the sacral chakra's transformative and creative power. The heart is essentially in the center of the chest, as is the thymus gland, which is key for immunity. The energy center that needs our attention for the sake of what we are exploring in this book is the third eye chakra, located in the center of the forehead, just above the eyes. The third eye chakra is connected to the pineal gland, a somewhat misunderstood brain structure that is crucial not only to dreams and dreaming but also to waking up the human consciousness into a much more direct connection with the divine.

The primary function of the pineal gland is to produce the hormone melatonin. In the simplest of explanations, the pineal gland produces a hormone that inspires us to fall asleep, so every night at a particular time, the pineal amps up production of this chemical and we feel sleepy. It is, of course, much more complex than that, for the pineal is also how we relate to light, so this activation is fueled not by the gland itself, but by its response to diminishing sunlight, signaling to the pineal that sleep is near and it's time to pump out some melatonin. This is why people are encouraged to limit screen time in the hours leading up to bed, for the generous amount of light that these devices pour on us keeps the pineal from recognizing that the time for sleep has arrived. There is also a direct connection between the amount of melatonin your brain produces and developmental stages of life. Teenagers have a flood of melatonin at a later hour, hence their tendency to stay up late and wake up even later. Older adults produce less melatonin, resulting in the need for less sleep as we age. While the circadian rhythm that guides our sleep also connects to our experience of changing light through the seasons, it's the connection to the sleep cycle that is of interest to us, which leads us to the best-kept secret of the pineal gland: DMT.

Dimethyltryptamine (DMT) is a naturally occurring substance found in many plants and animals, including human beings. It is thought to be generated in the pineal gland, though it has been found in other places in the human body, including the cerebral spinal fluid. It is so common in the plant world that there are various vines and greenery with high concentrations that are brewed in a ceremonial tea that many people in the modern world are familiar with. Ayahuasca is made as a brew, like a tea, made from a particular vine, another shrub, and sometimes other plants. While this is used in ceremonial traditions in the Amazon basin, its use has grown widely elsewhere in the world. This is how most people who have either heard of DMT or worked with it in this way come into contact with this powerful substance. It can also be synthesized in a lab using a specific toad venom as the source material for a more powerful substance that is ingested by smoking.

The effect of DMT, when ingested in any form, is a powerful psychedelic experience that can loosen the bonds of three-dimensional reality, cause tremendous euphoria, and generate a profound sense of connection to the divine. People who have consumed ayahuasca report having mystical experiences and spiritual revelations regarding their purpose on the planet and the true nature of the universe, and deep insights into how to grow as a person. In fact, many people report profoundly therapeutic effects, especially when working with depression or personal trauma. DMT seems to play an important role in spiritual awakening in human beings.

I find it fascinating that the brain structure that is responsible for the fact that we sleep at all is also the seat of the most profound expansion of consciousness available to us. Generation of DMT by the pineal gland during REM sleep may be the very brain chemistry process that allows this experience to happen. It may even be possible that the miniscule amounts of DMT available to all of us are what helps generate the visual explosion that dreams are.

And Then It Happened

My personal experience of such a multidimensional dream happened a few days after my thirty-fourth birthday, but in some ways this story starts in the year leading up to that. All that year, I had been captivated by the notion of being the auspicious age of thirty-three, known to foster the beginnings of a spiritual awakening. This age is featured prominently in the Christ mythology, as he was this age when he culminated his human journey. There is an astrological transit that everyone moves through at thirty-three that relates to the movement of Uranus through the birth chart, and this is the planet through which we have the potential to wake up to higher levels of consciousness. Even in yogic traditions, this is a significant age at which a person will either propel themselves positively into the directions cultivated by the previous actions or begin a midlife crisis, taking them down in order to, hopefully, rise up to a higher potential through conflict. In numerology, thirty-three is a master number, reflecting the power of the divine trinity of creativity, and as such, it is an age when many people wake up to their inner potential.

The year when I was thirty-three was an interesting transitional time for me. My exterior life reflected some growing success in the business side of the entertainment industry. I had woken up my physical body by turning to exercise and fitness as central to my life, which was then, and continues to be almost three decades later, an enormously important element of my self-expression. I had begun my self-investigation in earnest, deeply engaged in therapy and diving into all sorts of processes, teachings, healing classes, workshops, and all manner of inner healing.

But truly, I was also feeling quite lost. I had finally reconciled myself to leaving my dream of being an actor behind me, but I also knew in my gut that something was still elusive to me. While I consciously enjoyed my growing success in the world of business and I was getting to know myself powerfully from the inside out, rumbling just below the surface was a real sense of uncertainty about what my life needed from me.

I had been so excited to turn thirty-three, and had assumed that the year ahead was going to bring me some much-needed clarity. So in many ways, my thirty-fourth birthday was a tremendous disappointment. I felt lost, I was confused about the work I was doing, and a relationship that I had been very hopeful would turn into something significant was clearly not going to, and I felt privately ashamed of the inner sense of loss I was experiencing. Part of my disappointment that year was due to the fact that the man I was seeing was not available to celebrate my birthday weekend, and the following Saturday, we spent the day and evening together as a kind of make-up experience. I was inwardly miserable that night because I was arguing with the reality of what my life was versus what I wanted it to be. After what might have been a lovely evening if I had allowed it to be, we both fell into a bit of a fitful night's sleep.

That night, there was a rip in the fabric of the collective consciousness. The date was August 30, 1997, and during the early hours of August 31, Princess Diana was killed in Paris. I am convinced that this world event was partially responsible for the experience I had on a personal level while I slept. By the time I woke up, Gregg was already watching the endless news cycle on the television about this tragic event, which meant that while I was in the dream space, the world was being hit with a lightning bolt of change that would have a deep and lasting impact on the collective. In that numinous and liminal space, I had the following dream experience.

This happened during the last REM cycle of the night. Whatever chaotic dreams I may have been having gave way to something that was profoundly different from any other dream

I had ever had in my life, before or since. I had certainly had lucid experiences in dreams in the past, and this was like that but also unlike those moments. I have had profoundly lucid experiences in dreaming (see chapter 2) where the sensation in the dream state was exactly like waking life, but this was not that either. The setting was dreamy, and felt like a dream. There was something about the space I found myself in that was not at all like the chaotic, ever-changing dream landscapes that pepper most sleeping phenomena.

I was sitting in a boat on a lake. If I wanted to make an association with a waking-life setting, it seemed like a kind of rowboat where two people could sit facing each other. The lake was natural, pristine, and quite verdant, but it also had this very ethereal quality, like it wasn't quite life on Earth. It looked exactly like a natural setting, but amplified in every way. The colors were like in nature, but unnaturally vibrant. The peaceful and still water was flat and reflective, but at the same time, the stillness of the water seemed preternatural. And sitting across from me in the rowboat was the most beautiful woman I had ever seen.

I knew I was dreaming, so in that sense, this was a lucid dream, but it was more than just that I was aware that I was dreaming. I was aware that I was not in a typical dream space, where we are visiting an inner world of chaos within our psyche. This felt like an actual space, a multidimensional plane, where my sense of reality was opening up to something, well, other. In retrospect, with decades of wisdom with which to perceive this event, I can identify it as a multidimensional experience, where my entire being was connecting and directly interacting with something much, much bigger than my human, three-dimensional consciousness.

We had a conversation, this beautiful lady of the lake and I, though it was not like waking life, and so the experience of the dream itself was pure stillness and grace. Inside of the telepathic connection, I was given a few very clear ideas. One was that she was some sort of divine guide. Another was a very clear message that this was the only time she was ever going to be able to make her presence known to me in any direct sort of way. The last thing I was able to take from this exchange was this sort of promise that no matter where my life might take me, ultimately all was well, I was guided and protected, and this meeting was to somehow ground this into my perception of my life.

After this dream, I slipped out of REM and into sleep paralysis, which is a phenomenon of sleep covered extensively in chapter 6. While sleep paralysis is a frequently occurring experience in dreaming, this was the only experience I have ever had of it, which I find fascinating considering the potential mystical state that this sensation heralds. Falling into a hypnopompic hallucination right after being in a dream experience of multidimensional connection is not unrelated. The private experience that I was having was happening simultaneously with an enormous world event that was unfolding as I was still in my bed sleeping. It seems possible to me that I was able to have such a powerful inner experience because the outside world was also moving through a powerful transformative experience. In other words, because the fabric of the collective consciousness was already being ripped open by an enormous event, my personal consciousness was able to take advantage of that, delivering to me a beautiful mystical dream experience that I might not oth-erwise have been able to perceive.

Now, I wish I could tell you that this guide has always been in my psyche since I was introduced to it during this life-changing experience some twenty-five years ago, but that is not the case. In fact, I have often had a sense of envy for people whose inner phe-nomena allow them to connect to their guides in a very direct way. This is not the case for me. Although I feel the channeling of divine wisdom every time I listen to a dream or engage in a pri-vate session, or even when I am writing, this divine lady of the lake does not speak to me in any sort of direct way. One of the things I have had to do for myself over the last quarter of a cen-tury is find ways to relate to this powerful feminine guidance without that direct mental connection. Of course, I have evolved tremendously over that period of time, and the founda-tion of my entire spiritual practice is based on developing and deepening my personal connection with the divine feminine, and all that that concept might represent.

The Mystical, Magical Truth: The Divine as You Know It

When I started to do research for this book, I knew that one of the people I wanted to sit down with for a deep conversa-tion about their dreaming experience was a man I have known for almost two decades now. Eli is what I would call a modern urban mystic. In his seventies now, he has spent the bulk of his life in pursuit of spiritual understanding and attempting to live in oneness with existence itself. While he and I have had very different paths of focus, we both began connecting to powerful existential dreams at around three years old. We met to speak about his experience of mystical dreams, but before we dove into that discussion, Eli shared a mystical dreamlike experience that happened to him in his mid-twenties and was the foundation of his spiritual journey. In fact, all of the mystical dreaming experiences that he has had over the years ultimately spiral back to this wild phenomenon that came through him over fifty years ago.

A vision like I am about to describe is not unlike a dream experience, and this can be more understandable when you consider the brain and the pineal gland's capacity to generate DMT. As you have learned, when the conscious mind diminishes in power because we are in sleep mode, the pineal gland is already activated by virtue of helping generate the mechanism of sleep to begin with. With that perception at a very low volume, the powerful imagery of dreams is likely related to the presence of DMT in the system, causing the profound visual aspect of dreaming. But the pineal gland can also generate dreamlike mystical experiences during wakefulness. This is more likely to happen to someone older who has put a lot of resources toward opening up their spiritual nature. There are people who organically have an amplified experience of what the pineal gland can generate, and there are moments when conscious perception diminishes, the DMT bursts, and a human being can have a profoundly visual dreamlike experience in waking life. Eli had such an experience that jump-started his spiritual journey.

Eli began writing down his dreams in 1971, when he was in his early twenties. Six years later, the lid burst off his three-dimensional, limited self in a powerful expansion moment that was pure vision. Living in Brooklyn at the time, Eli decided to take a walk, but as he was sitting on the edge of his bed, his consciousness began to recede, and he quite suddenly and powerfully began to see what he interpreted as a gigantic disc sitting at the top of his head. Waves of energy and light were moving from the outer edges of this disc toward the center where his head was in an undulating oscillation pattern that Eli recognized as the universe itself sitting above him, putting his mind and perception at the center of the energetic structure.

Before long, Eli heard a voice. It seemed to be coming from this disc, and it simply said, "Hello." But it wasn't just the word hello; it was the word hello being expressed in every possible, conceivable language from every culture on the planet, and even voices and languages from every other planet in the universe that has conscious life. The voice was undeniably female, and for the first part of the vision, this greeting waved itself over and over again, rippling from the edges of this disc back to the center, which is where he and his body were. And it simply said, "Hello." There, a back-and-forth conversation arose, which Eli described like this:

"Hello," the voice says.

"Who are you?" I reply.

"You know who I am" is her retort.

"I don't," I say, completing the loop of a conversation that repeats a few times.

After about the third time through this exchange, I realize, "Oh my God, this is God. And she is speaking to me, but I ask her again, I've already figured that out. And when these waves come in, it's the most thunderous sound of golden luminous light pouring into my body."

She says, "You know who I am. I am the Great Mother. I am that from which all things come."

This visionary waking dream was the start of Eli's journey as a modern mystic. He has been interacting with this avatar for almost half a century now, and describes many moments of his life as including channeling moments with his energy, where he almost feels like he is taking dictation from this energy. Those channeled messages have been collected by Eli in a book he calls *God Waves*, harkening back to the waving energy of his original vision.

I asked Eli to recount the most powerful mystical dream he had ever had, and much to my surprise, it was something that happened quite recently. It also harkened back so powerfully to that spiritual awakening moment from five decades prior that one cannot appreciate the significance of this recent dream without drawing a line back to Eli's first encounter with the Great Mother.

I'm sitting in a classroom, but it might be on Zoom. I don't remember. And the teacher asks me for my interpretation of the poem that she just read to us, or we just read together in the class. And I find myself merging with an almost blinding gold, golden light. So again, for me, golden light spirals back to what happened in 1977. I'm sitting in the dream merging with this golden light, which is God: she. And part of me in the dream is panicking, thinking, "Is this a real mystical experience? Am I dreaming this dream in a class, or am I having an epileptic seizure or something?"

In all of these overlapping perceptions, Eli was dreaming, but he was lucid. He was in a classroom, but in a dream. He was waking up, but he was asleep. He was merging with this golden light and was captivated by a vision, but he also might have been having a seizure. In that in-between space that sometimes rises up as we are coming out of deep sleep, Eli realized that he was in fact dreaming, not having a seizure, and was actually having a powerful spiritual experience that he had never had in the dream state, not in over fifty years of voracious dreaming and waking-life spiritual practice. As he came more fully into wakefulness, he found himself singing a song that was prominent in his life in his twenties, so clearly his unconscious was tethering back to the big opening that sparked his spiritual journey all those years ago.

Many mystical dream experiences involve energies that are clearly feminine in nature. Adriana described her dream experience in this way:

I was dreaming something (don't know what) when I saw an amazingly beautiful woman at the center of the earth. She was surrounded by a circle of sparkling white opalescent light. An enormous funnel-type shape was pointed right at the opalescent sphere, and I seemed to be filling the funnel. She explained that this funnel contains the flow of all the thoughts, feelings, and beliefs that don't serve me. And she let me know that through her immense love for me and everyone, she absorbs (and wants) me/us to continue to send her this type of energy. And we all have to do it on our own in order for it to get to her. I felt an unimaginably pure love that I had never known. Clearly, she loves us, everyone.

This was a life-changing experience for Adriana. After she had the dream, the shift in her was absolute, and from that moment she understood that she didn't have to carry around or keep any of the emotional and psychological patterns that were not serving her. It is one thing to know this as an intellectual idea, but a much more powerful experience when we learn that there is this huge energy of love and containment that we are held in. This was the first time that Adriana connected to this energy in her dream state, but the sense of connection to this power has never left her and can still generate beautiful feelings inside her. Through this relationship, Adriana is able to surrender and release troubling moments to the care of this loving, embracing divine feminine energy.

Connecting to the divine feminine is our birthright, and in fact Adriana described connecting with the goddess Gaia in her dream. Gaia is a Latin word that means "Earth," and in Greek traditions she was an actual goddess. Gaia was a primordial goddess, and was the personification of the Earth. The primordial deities were not given human characteristics, nor were they worshiped like their later counterparts. They were more abstract, and Gaia was the goddess that might be considered the Earth herself.

Here is an experience from Dianna, who described what she called "this beautiful female presence" that appeared in her dream. There was a sense that she was a representative of the universe itself. In the dream, there was a dark-blue star-filled sky in the background, while the image of this presence was just her head and face. Her face was also a striking color, a deep royal blue, with huge almond-shaped black eyes. Dianna describes locking eyes with this figure in the dream, and the soft, peaceful gaze of this figure generated the sensation that a blessing was being bestowed upon her. This image has stayed with Dianna ever since, and has allowed her to feel an ongoing connection to the divine in the years since the dream.

Here is an experience featuring the archetypal Wise Woman, shared with me by dreamer Georgina. Many of these dream experiences start out as standard dreams, and since we are in a state of energetic receptivity, we leave the dream space and enter multidimensional space. As Georgina reports, "At some point I realized I was in a spiritual event." At this event, she was being ushered toward an opportunity to meet this figure of divine wisdom, and she was filled with a sense of profound gladness. After Georgina introduced herself, the Wise Woman put her hands on Georgina's back and began filling her with an incredible energy, something that she had never experienced before or since. In the dream state itself, Georgina became a bit lucid and likened the initiatory process she was experiencing to feeling like how she imagined it must have felt to be touched by a saint. Like anyone who has reported such a dream to me, Georgina has never forgotten it, and the image of the dream experience has stayed vibrantly with her as a source of comfort and connection.

Sibila was a woman in her fifties at the time of this writing. Back in the summer of 1990, when she was twenty-four years old, she completed her master of laws degree from Copenhagen. This time of her life was challenging on a number of levels, but at the center of her struggles was the fact that she hated law school and had, ultimately, no real interest in becoming an attorney. That was her mother's dream, and the twenty-some-thing-year-old Sibila had not yet developed the sovereignty of self that would have allowed her to have more agency over her adult life. That all changed with a powerful dream, one that fits the description of a life-changing visit with a mystical dimension of consciousness.

The year following graduation was chaotic for Sibila. She was busy in her professional sphere, attempting to carve out a career in a field that she had a deep aversion to. A personal romantic relationship was problematic, and those problems were growing. She sought help in therapy and found herself a psychotherapist who, quite fortunately, had a bit of a spiritual bent, which worked well with Sibila's burgeoning spiritual sensibility. During this difficult year, supported in therapy, Sibila began a deep self-investigation that would be the basis of how she would live the rest of her life.

The theme of Sibila's work had to do with facing a dare: Daring to be herself. Daring to walk out of law. Daring to leave her entire life behind her and travel. Daring not to be in the current romantic relationship that was, ultimately, holding her back. After some time, Sibila found herself in the rather difficult position of being on both sides of this continuum. She felt a sense of audacity rising up in her, which could help her strike out on her own, but she was also finding fear rising up in equal measure, which was holding her back. She was also being undermined by financial limitations that kept her from hopping on a plane to make a radical shift happen.

Then everything changed with a dream.

Really, it was more of a dream experience, which is an accurate way of describing it. Such dreams are so radically different from those in the typical dream space that they are reported by people to be more of an "experience" than a dream. This is how Sibila described this multidimensional moment:

> I saw myself quite young, lying on my deathbed. A being of light was with me, sitting at the left side of the bed. This being had no gender, felt like a guide or a guardian angel who was totally understanding and compassionate. The sorrow I saw myself feel and be in on the deathbed was immense and unbearable. More sorrow than I had ever felt. The being of light simply asked me, "Do you want this?"

Shortly after this dream, Sibila faced the biggest fears she was struggling with at that time. Her paralyzing fears and discontent kept her from taking risks, which included traveling and making big choices that might be frightening and leave her vulnerable, but without which her life would stay very small. This dream experience kept rising up in her mind until, two months later, she purchased an open-ended ticket to San Francisco. Despite her debts and those previously debilitating fears, she hopped on that plane, and her life has felt like hers ever since.

Sibila knew that she had received a powerful gift that night. She recognized the experience itself as something far more powerful than just her brain engaging in the rapid-fire activity of a typical dream. In fact, this experience imprinted in her consciousness in a way that has impacted her ever since. There have been other moments like this in the decades since that first experience, where not only do these light beings have a sense of personal agency, but the environment in which they live has structure. Sibila describes these spaces as being like great halls in which these beings dwell. Several times over the course of her life she has received important guidance through such nighttime experiences, though none have been quite as vivid as that first initiatory meeting with her guides.

Here is a dream that operated like an instruction manual for change, transformation, healing, and growth. Kari shared this dream, which changed the course of her life and marked a significant opening in her spiritual practice and how she approaches moving through life. She described a dream where she found herself flying. As she glanced down, she noticed that the shadow that she was making on the ground revealed that she had wings, as if to symbolically represent the notion that we are always operating in two dimensions, and the spiritual underpinnings of our experience are, ultimately, part of the invisible world.

As the dream progressed, Kari landed on the ground and found herself in the company of what she described as an angel: "She was beautiful, but not in that goddess sort of way. She was more simple and plain sweetness, so to speak. She had light-brown curly hair and was wearing a dress that seemed like something maybe a milkmaid would wear." This image reminds me of the power of the feminine in all things, as this figure was the conduit to a powerful archetypal energy that was key to Kari's sense of personal growth, integration, and coming into wholeness in a life devoted to healing and self-actualization. This first deeply feminine energy rose up in the dreamworld to connect with Kari, but it was a very masculine power that was downloaded into Kari as a result of this dream.

Kari's angel indicated that she was there to make an introduction. She went on to say, "I am introducing you to the Archangel of Fire."

At this point, out of a smoldering forest the trees were all burnt. Just the trunks were left black and gray with smoke, and smoke still coming up off the ground. Everything was gray and black, but nothing was actually burning any longer. Out of this he came, wearing a purple velvet suit. Reminded me of something maybe Prince would wear. He was tall and well-built.

If fire is symbolic of all change, and life itself is nothing more than a series of changes, little mini deaths and rebirths all throughout life, then the setting here tells us that we are in the presence of an existential energy that connects to this process of change that we as human beings must all grapple with. The color purple is related to high levels of spiritual consciousness. The addition of an aspirational character in the form of Prince was likely helping Kari identify with this energy at a personal level. She went on to describe the dream in great detail.

With him was a legion. The legion wasn't marching; they were more free with their movements, more acrobatic. He introduced himself and told me not to be scared or worried about the smoke, that it would not hurt me. He said, "I want to show you something." I went with him through the smoldering forest to a place that the area around was more green. There was what seemed like a glass box or sort of enclosed box with a window with a man inside. The archangel asked me, "What do you notice?" I examined the man and the situation. He was sitting inside and had a wound on his leg/knee area that was big and oozing with green and yellow puss. He was fixated on it and kept picking and digging at it. I looked around the room and noticed a small folded-up note. I opened the note and read it. It was from his mom, telling him that she loved him. He said, "It doesn't matter." I looked at him again and said, "Yes, it does matter." His knee was now healing. The puss was now only on the edges, and the center was now red and starting to close. He still couldn't see the benefit, but I could. This was the end of the dream. It felt very surreal and very profound to me.

The meaning of this dream is simple. It basically declares that love is the healer. There is the old adage "Time heals all wounds," but this is inaccurate. Only love can heal wounds. Time comes into play only when there is a need for time to pass in order for someone to allow love to come in and do the healing.

This dream really does feel instructive to me. Kari was being shown, quite literally, how we work with wounds, and eventually we allow love to come into the mix, and then healing can rise up and transform any wound. In Kari's words, this dream clarified something that is indeed a staple in a modern psycho-spiritual practice: "The intention of where you put your focus and the ability of love to heal. I believe this was part of the message to assist others to heal and also that I have protection to go where I need to go."

Very often, the mystical dream is initiatory, where the appearance of the dream at a relatively early age in life has a profound impact on the journey of the dreamer. Krista is a woman in her early forties now who makes her living as a spiritual life coach and medium. She understood her gifts in a private way long before she was ready to "come out the spiritual closet," as she likes to joke. The following dream rose up a number of years ago, and marked the transition between her being someone with intuitive gifts and her sharing those gifts in a significant way by offering her services to a vibrant clientele.

> I was in the middle of a beautiful massive field. There was a giant statue figure of a Human King (Indian descent) that had mystical attributes to him (had extra limbs) and it was made of gold. It felt imposing, powerful, and wrong at the same time. Then all of a sudden, a battle erupted all around me from his side and another who opposed him, and chaos took over the serene field. Then I looked up to the heavens/sky and saw that there was another battle as well, this time between angels/light and demons/dark. So there I was standing in the middle, watching both battles simultaneously. Then an angel figure appeared right next to me and said, "This is your burden—to see and experience both earthly and heavenly battles." I just felt this sensation of acceptance, understanding, and support.

Krista woke from this dream experience and had a powerful sense that all would be well. At a time in her life where she was particularly vulnerable, she was able to tap into that invisible sense of support that comes when we deeply know and trust that our lives are held by much greater powers than our own small self. From that moment on, Krista has been unwavering in her journey toward being a spiritual medium, author, and teacher. Like many on this path, Krista's mystical dream experience became the anchor for everything that happened after it.

McKay is a man now in his early thirties, but after college, he moved to Los Angeles and found himself, in his words, "in a stage of huge life transition from college into some sort of post-undergrad adulting." This was also a time of being in the throes of massive internal emotional shifts, and one of the first things McKay did in his new hometown was connect with a healer. This healer was helping McKay move through some energetic stuckness, and this work was waking something up in him that would later reveal itself as a spiritual awakening, which, as we have come to see, often begins with a dream experience.

McKay was crashing on an air mattress at a friend's home at the time, and one day he fell asleep listening to a meditation. It is worth mentioning that this behavior of listening to meditation before bed, though currently the norm for McKay, was not something in his wheelhouse at the time, but circumstances inspired him on that fateful night to tune in to this meditative track as he was drifting off to sleep.

The dream started with just a sense of awareness, and through this awareness, McKay had the sense of rising above and away from the earth. From this higher vantage point, there were no visible signs of life below, no figures, people, or topography. McKay even reported having a sense that although it was him having this perceptive awareness, he was not even there in the dream. There was just this almost disembodied sense of awareness that he understood to be his own watching, his own witnessing. In this very far distance from Earth, McKay was in a space that he described as infinite, very dark, with a blackness that was an absence of light. It was recognizable as an imagined sense of outer space, but McKay understood that it was even beyond that notion, beyond space, and in a place that was infinitely beyond outer space, though even that description is a mind-bending idea. Within this impossible sense of the infinite nature of existence itself, McKay had the following experience of perception.

And in the infinite space (which also felt not far away at all, but RIGHT THERE), I saw massive ribbons of energy moving in many, many colors. Slowly. Massively. Like nothing I had ever experienced. They were huge. Mighty. Megawatt. Beyond. WHALES of energy and color and light twirling, dancing. Moving. Slow. I want to use the word "powerful," but the word totally falls flat. I don't have words for it. Something like the Northern Lights, but so beyond that, not of Earth, astral energy on a scale like nothing I can really describe—MASSIVE—with a depth and profundity words can't touch. A heft like nothing I'd ever felt before, an everything-ness, liquid light moving with the weight of worlds but somehow totally light. Made of lightness. And though the scale was infinitely beyond me, I experienced it as right there. Immediate. Intimate. Within me. But also "me" is incorrect—because I DIDN'T EXIST. I was just a watching-ness. A witness. And it was INFINITE. So, I'm seeing outer space, far away from Earth, and I'm watching light and energy move in this wild psychedelic trip for the ages. But it didn't feel psychedelic or imaginary—it was just fuckin' real.

When McKay woke up, it took him a while to remember that he was in his friend's living room in West Hollywood, California. Even after he rose from the air mattress to visit the toilet in typical morning fashion, it still took a few beats for him to return to an awakened state. He slowly began to let the dream reality slip away, and just as it did so, he heard a phrase: "Soul Space."

Chapter Nine

Sleep Hygiene

Sleep hygiene is a term that relates to approaching your experience of retiring for the day with some conscious awareness. Our days are more complicated than ever, and many people transition from their waking life to sleepy time without much of a thought. This, of course, has led to tremendous challenges with sleep and sleeping that can actually be transformed by how you approach this part of your day. It is widely understood that screen time on your devices before sleep can inhibit sleep from coming, because the light stimulates the pineal gland, telling the brain that it is daytime. By limiting screen time before bed, people find that they fall asleep with greater ease. This is just one element of what sleep hygiene is. If you pay attention to how you transition from your waking life to your sleep experience, and add a sense of ritual designed to make the experience more sacred, then you are practicing what I refer to as sleep hygiene.

I have a compelling need to straighten up my house before bed. When I was in college at nineteen, I met a man who was, at that time, the most spiritually driven young person I had ever met. I went to his room one day and was struck by how neat it was, how precisely his bed was made, and the sense of pristine stillness I felt when I entered his space, considering most college students live more often in squalor than not. After giving me a book on St. Francis that he thought I would be inspired by, he responded to my adulations about the cleanliness of his space. "I always want my home to be in a state of readiness to receive" is what he said to me. And here he was, receiving me in his space, and I, in fact, felt a certain kind of way because his space did indeed feel energetically inviting.

This exchange transformed me, and from that moment on, I have related to this idea of having my home be in constant readiness to receive others. I have a similar experience of my bed, in that I always make my bed in the morning, because I want my bed in a state of readiness to receive my body as I lie down each night to experience the sweet death of sleep. When I am getting ready to head to bed, it is very natural for me to look around my house and make sure that everything is put away and in its place, and if there is something that needs to be cleaned, it is done. When I then head into my bedroom, I have a sense of peace because my home is in a state of readiness in the way that I prefer, and I embrace the yumminess of my ready bed. I refer to this preparation for sleep as sleep hygiene: *sleep*, because of course we are talking about this daily need we have, and *hygiene*, because the cleaner we are in this process and the more sacredly we view and inhabit it, the more likely we are to cultivate and develop a richer experience of sleep and dreaming.

Dreamer Kathy is on board with the tech-free bedroom and has made sure her bedroom is free of radiating energy by having no television setup in the room where she sleeps. Her cell phone is not welcome in her bedroom, though she cleverly leaves it on, but in another room, in case there should be some middle-of-the-night emergency and someone needs to reach her. She does, however, keep a low-tech cassette player—very old-school—so that she can listen to music or other relaxing material with technology that doesn't put waves of radiation into the bedroom. She also keeps other tools at the ready in case of evenings where sleep is evasive.

> My goal is to read for thirty minutes prior to going to bed, but that doesn't always happen because I'm too tired to focus. Sometimes I write my to-do list, so it's not "weighing" on my brain and I can let go of that, knowing I can pick it up in the morning. Often I'll select a crystal to hold or have near me while I do my daily Reiki and/or meditation; lights out for Reiki/meditation. Once I get comfy and ready to drift off to la-la land, I say some gratitude statements, especially if I'm angry, resentful, jealous, sad, or disappointed.

Michele is a woman who began her research into dreaming experiences when she was a teenager and reports that major periods of her adult life that included intense personal growth also included intensified dream experiences. Over the years, besides various prayers and mantras that have worked for her, she has also actively taken advantage of the internet, where there is a plethora of guided meditations, binaural beat recordings, and sound healing tracks that are freely available through various websites. Specific crystals, such as black tourmaline and black obsidian, have been found by Michele to be effective as an energetic amplifier, leading to deeper sleep and more powerful REM cycle experiences. She has always kept a very clean sleeping environment, both in terms of her bedroom itself and with regard to her media consumption as she gets closer to bedtime.

Jeanette takes her sleeping environment to a whole other level. Her bedroom has one tourmaline pyramid on each side of the bed, and the bed itself is outfitted with wands made of selenium, crystals that are perfect for energetic protection. She and her partner will often burn sage or other incense, put on some high-frequency music, and drift off to sleep. She has a prayer at the ready: "May nothing but good come to me and may nothing but good come from me in the name of Mother Father God. Therefore, it is done." As she says this prayer, she visualizes a golden three-dimensional pyramid around the bed, and in that prayerful state, she might focus on releasing attachments to others, or put crystals beneath her pillow on days when the energy around her feels particularly amplified.

Elizabeth finds that singing childhood songs in her head has become a natural way that she connects to gratitude, and while she doesn't use this specific word, she told me that this experience is something like a prayer. For Lisa, the experience is a focus on the physical, where she pictures her body relaxing as she imagines deep relaxation going to where her mind is focused. Karin has studied mystical energy for many years, and shared a relaxation technique that I had never heard of but that sounds pretty powerful. This may take a great deal of energetic sensitivity to accomplish. Karin focuses on attempting to feel her heartbeat in one of her big toes. While this took years to master, she claims that the resulting relaxation that arises from doing this is just extraordinary, and I am inclined to believe her.

In this final chapter, we will explore different ways to set you up for a deeper, more integrated experience of dreaming, including things you can do in your waking life, as well as how to approach bedtime and your sleep experience with greater reverence.

Meditation

I cannot emphasize this enough: If you desire a greater connection to your dream life, and a deepening of the intuitive potential of the human instrument, you need to have a meditation practice. In fact, if you are reading this book and you don't have a meditation practice, close this book, go get one on meditation (or search online), and start learning a technique that speaks to you. Who you are and how you think are not the same thing. Meditation—and this refers to all meditation practices—is designed to help us tap more directly into the center of our being, and generate less reliance on the thoughts we are thinking that help us understand our identity.

Conscious awareness and thinking are related, but they are not the same thing. Your identity through your conscious awareness is like the center of you, the "I Am" of who you know yourself to be. You might think of this as Self with a capital *S*. And then you have thoughts. So many thoughts. Never-ending thoughts that, unfortunately, wind up captivating you, so much so that you think you *are* the thoughts you are having. But you are not.

We are these magnificent beings, largely unconscious, completely underpinned by a multidimensional experience that is the organic and natural way to exist. And we have this mechanism that helps us navigate this mysterious realm. Meditation, any technique of meditation, is designed, ultimately, to train and discipline your thoughts so that you have an experience of self rise up more powerfully. This happens when you find ways to feel the connection to your wholeness and recognize your thoughts as something that is added to the system so that you can see where you're going but not much beyond that.

This leads many people to incorrectly imagine that meditation is successful only when the mind is quiet, but that is not at all accurate. Meditation is successful when you begin to make the distinction between your thinking and the spaces between your thoughts. This is accomplished mostly by focusing on some neutral idea, such as the breath, a mantra, or a phrase. Even staring at a candle or other object can be a powerful point of reference. We start with an intention, and for this example, let's use focusing on a simple mantra as the meditation technique. You sit for a prescribed amount of time with the intention of saying to yourself over and over again, "All is well." Of course, the thinking mind will interfere, which is natural and organic. We allow for this, and then gently turn the mind back to the intended mantra. It is in the noticing of the thoughts grabbing your attention, and the willingness to turn back to the mantra, that meditation becomes what it is.

It is accurate to say that over time, a disciplined meditator is going to enjoy clearer thoughts during the act of meditation, but the end game is not the quietude of the mind, but rather the discipline to notice when that quietude has been taken hostage by thoughts and then return to the intended focus. That's what makes a meditation practice a success. If, during a twenty-minute sit, you spent most of that time thinking, but in fact did successfully notice this and bring your attention back to your mantra a few times, that is a successful meditation. People with naturally more chaotic thinking will often try meditation, have this experience of a crowded mind, and then declare that meditation doesn't work and is not for them.

There are so many ways to meditate, and all of them will help you begin to discipline your mind. You could explore until you find a way that speaks to you, or you could approach it the way I do and have a number of techniques and choose whatever feels right in the present moment. If you recall, it is this interfering thinking mind that goes to sleep when we do. This is why our dreams so easily lead us to mystical experiences—because there are no crowded thoughts to distract us from the more powerful, but much more subtle, energies of perception. Meditating to cultivate a quiet mind is a muscle, which, in sleep, does not need to be worked. But working that muscle in our waking life is completely transformative. A mind that is more spacious, open, and disciplined with regard to thinking is also more open to mystical experiences while we are awake, and that discipline will follow us into sleep. For a life with a greater connection to the mystery of consciousness, it doesn't matter how you meditate, only that you do.

Remembering Your Dreams

Everybody dreams, and we dream every time we move through a sleep cycle. We don't always remember our dreams readily, and some people are not wired to easily connect in waking life with material that was exposed during dreams. When people say to me, "I don't dream," they really mean that they have no recollection of dreaming. Here's an oversimplified reason why this is true. We are visual creatures, and most human beings experience everything about their conscious awareness through sight.

There is a section in the brain that is designed to interpret outside energy and convert it into visual stimuli that allow us to understand who, where, and when we are existing. Imagine a line going from light outside of you, through your eyes, and to a particular section of the brain used for sight. Dreams are visual, and powerfully so, but the areas of the brain that are "seeing" the dream do not include the visual cortex associated with our eyes. Once consciousness fires up, that dream perception starts to be diminished by the much louder conscious awareness, and of course if we open our eyes, we are flooded with data that we must interpret, and that subtle imagery that our brain was holding in the dream state can evaporate before our conscious awareness can even begin to perceive it.

Some people are more naturally wired for this distinction of perception to happen simultaneously enough that they wake up each morning with the potential of remembering their dreams, and vividly. For many folks, that dream memory is not constant, and for some, it has never been felt as something active. Fortunately, you can encourage dream memory by using the following techniques.

First, the intention to remember your dreams has to be strong. This chapter is filled with ways to ritualize and focus your intentions for a deeper experience of your dreams. Remember how powerful setting the intention to remember your dreams can be, and generating ritualized context for this intention can be a strong trigger to the unconscious that you desire a greater conscious relationship with that mysterious realm. Set the intention before bedtime every evening that you will remember your dreams.

Of course, if you don't have a way to record your dreams at the ready, you will interrupt the subtle dream memory frequency, so having your dream journal right by your bedside is key. In this modern age of technology, many people prefer using a recording device to speak their dreams as they rouse, and there is nothing wrong with that. I am a bit old-school, and I believe that putting pen to paper is a more visceral act and will help the unconscious material blend into your conscious awareness through writing in a way that speaking out loud may circumnavigate. However, at the end of the day, the important thing here is proximity and not being too interrupted between waking and going to the means of recording your dream content.

The magic action is this. Write something (or record something) every day no matter what, even if what you say is, "I don't recall any dreams from last night." Then wait a moment to see if anything rises up before you turn away from this desire. This is important, and it's a bit mysterious in how it works. This language tells your unconscious that you are ready and willing for more information to come through, and it will respond in kind.

I have heard stories where a person's dream recall went from zero to sixty in just a week or so of practicing this technique.

The Power of Good Sleep

The quality of the sleep you get counts. Deep, restful sleep requires a level of relaxation in the body, quietude in the mind, and the uninterrupted opportunity to go through the entire sleep cycle at least three or four times. Stress, poor nutrition, and neglecting your body from a health and fitness perspective can all inhibit the deep, relaxing sleep needed to restore the body each night through sleep. The body, including the brain, has an innate intelligence to accomplish this, and the more we can support the body to do what it is designed to do, the more we benefit.

Supplements and Nutrition: There are natural sleep aids, such as melatonin, and herbal substances that induce relaxation, such as valerian root and kava kava. Some research suggests that magnesium in the system also helps sleep come with greater ease. Mugwort is a plant that is thought to increase the relaxation that leads to deep sleep and increased vividness of dreaming. While not all natural remedies are backed by science, anything that enhances the sleep experience is valuable to assist you in your quest for more powerful dream experiences. In the tradition of Ayurveda, jatamansi is another plant that is used medicinally for sleep enhancement.

Medications: Many medications have an impact on sleep and dreaming, so make sure you are aware of the side effects of any medication you are taking. Sleep medications such as Ambien are a class of drug that can generate tremendous side effects, such as increased nightmares and a tendency to sleepwalk. Cannabis is often used to induce sleep, but it can also eradicate the ability to remember dreams upon waking.

Electronics: Keeping your bedroom free of electrical equipment is ideal for a clean sleeping space, so it is best to keep your computer router as far away from the bedroom as possible, and the room itself should be as free of such technology as is possible based on the physical layout of your home. Since sleep itself is generated by the pineal gland, which responds directly to light, decreasing screen time is crucial for good sleep, so do your best to limit your exposure to such bright light at least one hour before you go to bed. Additionally, and especially if you consider yourself empathic or energetically sensitive, it is a good idea to refrain from taking in social media or scrolling through your newsfeed before bed.

Guided Meditations: Guided meditations can be a powerful relaxation method, and for those who don't find it distracting, this can be a powerful way to increase readiness to fall into a deep and restful sleep. The internet is filled with such tracks, so exploring this is just a click away. There has also been tremendous research on the impact of certain frequencies of sound, and what is called *binaural beats*, where rather than words guiding you into a more relaxed state, the sounds and rhythms themselves act powerfully on the brain, enhancing relaxation and the depth of sleep.

Crystals: Many people incorporate working with crystals into their sleep experience, either by placing objects under their pillow or even wearing items that won't get tangled during sleep. The frequency of the crystal can have a subtle but definitive impact on energy, relaxation, and the ability to fall asleep easily.

Other Interventions: Masturbation is a fantastic mechanism for relaxation and can often help people release the energy of the day and flood the body with a well-being chemical bath. Orgasm is a natural sleep aid. Physically relaxing the body is a great way to cut through some of the stress that can interfere with relaxation in bed, so literally stretching before bed is not only good for sleep, but can easily fit into a practice of pre-sleep ritual. Progressive relaxation is an effective meditative approach to calming the body. You use your mind's eye to picture your physical body, part by part, usually starting with the feet and working up. As you picture each body part in your mind, that body part will automatically relax, increasing well-being and facilitating good sleep.

Sleep Time as Ritual: There is a power to ritual that is transcendent. It starts with intention, as everything must. If your intention is to have a deeper, more rich and powerful experience of the mystical nature of your dreaming life, then there is a huge distinction between having that idea as a passive desire and turning that idea into a powerful intention through ritual and declaration. All of the items listed above are ways to change how you view the process of going from waking life to what I call the sweet death of sleep. When we approach this daily experience of sleep with intention and focus, we are more likely to approach everything else in our life with the same level of conscious awareness, intention, and focus, and the life that emerges from this level of living in the flow is one of purpose and meaning.

Conclusion

Life is a mystery, and one of the most beautiful ways to live an extraordinary life is to have some relationship with this mystery. There are happy accidents that make our solar system an extraordinary place, and one of the mechanisms built into this system is the binary of day and night. The Earth spins, and we split our world into the side bathed in sunlight on the one hand and the infinite plunge into darkness that the other half is experiencing along the way. We don't know why life in a physical body needs to switch between wakefulness and sleep, but it does, and sleep is perhaps the most profound mystery of how life in a body works.

We seek the light and fear the dark, yet we are exposed to this shadowy landscape every night of our lives. I sometimes refer to sleep and dreaming as the sweet death of sleep, for this is how we practice our ultimate death. If death is life's ultimate mystery, then dreams and dreaming are the most direct access we have to understanding all of life that is hidden from our conscious awareness. That mystery includes what we call the unconscious, where all of the real juice in life is held. While we are awake, our conscious awareness can keep our intuitive voice at bay. It's not called the still, small voice for nothing; intuitive information can be hard to hear. But when we release the hold that our thinking mind has on us, we tap more deeply into our intuition and the guidance that comes from the other side of consciousness.

To contemplate our dreams is to contemplate our divinity, and anything we might do to deepen the way we relate to our own divine nature always results in the potential to live in grace, ease, and a sense of flow. These pages have attempted to inspire you to understand that the best way to expand and grow your pre-installed intuitive nature is happening right there inside of you every time you go to sleep. We dream ourselves awake, and I trust that you are ready to take this idea to the next level of your personal development. As I like to say in my own waking life, *have at it!*

To Write to the Author

If you wish to contact the author or would like more information about this book, please write to the author in care of Llewellyn Worldwide Ltd. and we will forward your request. Both the author and the publisher appreciate hearing from you and learning of your enjoyment of this book and how it has helped you. Llewellyn Worldwide Ltd. cannot guarantee that every letter written to the author can be answered, but all will be forwarded. Please write to:

Dr. Michael Lennox
⅟ Llewellyn Worldwide
2143 Wooddale Drive
Woodbury, MN 55125-2989
Please enclose a self-addressed stamped envelope for reply,
or $1.00 to cover costs. If outside the U.S.A., enclose
an international postal reply coupon.

Many of Llewellyn's authors have websites with additional information and resources. For more information, please visit our website at http://www.llewellyn.com.

Notes

 **Notes**

Notes